The Border League Story

By Laing Speirs

**One Hundred Years
of the
World's Oldest Rugby League**

Price :- £8.99

© The Border League

First published in 2000 by

The Border League
c/o Scottish Borders Rugby Union
Channel House
Channel Street
Galashiels TD1 1BA

No part of this publication may be reproduced or transmitted in any form or by any means, electronic or mechanical, including photocopying, recording or otherwise, without the written permission of the publishers.

ISBN 0 9539677 0 0

Printed by Buccleuch Printers Ltd.
Carnarvon Street, Hawick

Contents

		Page
1.	Foreword - Lord Monro of Langholm, A.E., D.L.	v
2.	Acknowledgements	vii
3.	Message from Iain Fiddes, Head of Community Relations, Bank of Scotland	viii
4.	The Birth and Growth of the World's First Rugby League	1
5.	A Hundred Years in Borders Rugby	12
6.	The Clubs	

	Gala -	Successes and Near Misses	19
		The Game That Inspired a Song	27
	Hawick -	The Green Machine Rolls On	30
		Jim Renwick Ends Gala Hopes	38
	Jed-forest -	Successful Early Years	41
		Cheers, Tears, and Jethart's Here	47
	Langholm -	Single Win a Happy Memory	49
		Christy Elliot Makes Sure	53
	Melrose -	A Big Finish to the Century	56
		Top Form Melrose Take Trophy	64
	Carlisle -	The Cumberland Connection	66
	Selkirk -	Years of Waiting End in Success	70
		Archie Little Wraps Up League Trophy	74
	Kelso -	A Long Wait Well Worth While	77
		Cool Ker Sees Kelso Through	85
	Peebles -	Come Late and Win Early	87
		Happiness at The Gytes on a Friday Night	90

		Page
7.	Reflections	
	Darkie Smith - Memories of the Kelso Breakthrough	92
	Robin Charters - Old Values Still Needed in League's Future	94
	Derek Brown - Top Players Needed for the Game Tomorrow	98
	Graham Bateman - The Colourful Characters of Philiphaugh	100
	John Smail - A Few Border League Thoughts	103
	Jack Mitchell - Hopes and Fears for the Future of the League	105
	Bob Burrell and George Murray - The Lighter Side of the League	106
	Atholl Innes - Memories from the Cuttings Book	108
8.	Sponsors' Support for Borders Rugby	110
9.	The District League	111
10.	List of Presidents	113
11.	List of Secretaries and Treasurers.	113
12.	List of Border League Champions	114
13.	List of District League Champions	115

FOREWORD

by The Rt. Hon. Lord Monro of Langholm. A.E., D.L.

The Border League has stood the test of time. It is the oldest association of rugby union clubs who formed themselves into a league competition, and league table. Not only has it been a tremendous success in rugby terms, but it has brought our Border towns even closer together.

Maybe friendly rivalry is an understatement as our matches are always keenly fought, but always in the best of spirits. A little rough and tumble on the field always disappears afterwards in the clubhouse.

Whatever the ups and downs of Scottish rugby the Border League has never had any doubts about its continuation. It provides the hardest and most competitive rugby. There is no question that if Border rugby is doing well, then Scotland will do well. Border rugby is brimming with team spirit, an ingredient that is halfway or more to winning matches.

I first played in a Border League match in April, 1939 as a teenager, little thinking it would be October, 1946, before my next match for Langholm ! However all that lost time was made up, in coincidence, as president of the Border League when Langholm won the League and unofficial championship in 1959.

I am particularly pleased that in this centenary year of the Border League the presidency should fall to Jock Scott of my own club, Langholm, the oldest rugby club in the Borders.

I could not end a foreword without one word on my greatest love - the Border Sevens. We must never lose our birthright established at Melrose. We must keep pressing the S.R.U. to give sevens a higher priority.

Well done all the officials and players of the Border League. I know we will flourish in the years ahead.

Hector Monro

(signed) Lord Monro of Langholm

The original Border League Cup, first played for in 1906-7 and still competed for at the end of the century.

The Scottish Borders Council presented a special trophy to mark the first 100 years of the League competition in the Borders.

ACKNOWLEDGEMENTS

The preparation of this book was possible only with the co-operation of scores of rugby folk, including many club members who hunted through the archives, and who gave of their time to recall old stories and former days. The practical support of the Bank of Scotland was greatly appreciated.

The co-operation of the following former players, officials and supporters of the Border clubs was particularly valuable:

    Lord Monro of Langholm
    Jack Dun and Derek Brown of Melrose
    Walter Hume of Jed-forest
    Bill Jackson and Graham Bateman of Selkirk
    Ron Smith and Robin Charters of Hawick
    Jack Mitchell of Gala
    Donald Swanson of Peebles
    Norman Anderson and Allan Smith of Kelso
    Ronnie Tait of Langholm
    Norman Laycock and the late Tom Scott of Carlisle
    George Murray, Secretary and Treasurer of the Border League

The contributions of John Smail and Atholl Innes are gratefully acknowledged, as is the assistance in research provided by :

    Fiona White, Library Services Manager of the Scottish Rugby Union.
    The staff in the archives department of the Borders Library Service
    The Librarian at The Rugby Football Union, Twickenham.
    The Border League officials past and present.

Particular thanks are due to Allan McCredie of Hawick, whose computer skills have made the task of preparing this book so much easier, and to the staff of Buccleuch Printers for their advice and efficiency.

L.S.

✵ BANK OF SCOTLAND

Welcome to 'The Border League Story'

We hope you find this comprehensive record of the development and achievements of Borders Rugby both enjoyable and informative.

Bank of Scotland's sponsorship of the Border League is now in its 10th year and the Bank is extremely proud of its long association with rugby in the Borders. The League continues to be an integral part of Borders life and is to be congratulated on reaching its centenary year - a truly unique achievement in world rugby competition! Reaching this momentous milestone is, in no small measure, attributable to the dedication and enthusiasm of the League officials, the clubs and the rugby watching public.

As part of our commitment to the community and Scottish Rugby in the Borders we are proud to sponsor the Bank of Scotland Border League.

Iain Fiddes
Head of Group Community Relations
Bank of Scotland

THE BIRTH AND GROWTH OF THE WORLD'S FIRST RUGBY LEAGUE

The five Border rugby clubs who banded together to form the first competitive rugby league in the world had already been setting about each other for many years before they took their historic decision.

With strong links and even stronger rivalry well established they were able to blend their irregular games into a competition that became one of the longest lasting and most intense in Scottish amateur sport.

The teams of the Border valleys shared a common historical and geographical heritage, but to their chosen sport they added individual character and colour.

The founding fathers probably didn't know, and equally probably would not have cared very much, that they were creating a league which was not only the first in the rugby world, but the third oldest rugby union competition of any kind.

Only the Calcutta Cup, first played for in 1879, and the University Match, first played in 1872, are older than the competition which was put together in the Scottish Borders in 1901-2.

The first teams in the competition came from a hardy background where rugby had been played with fire and passion for many years.

It wasn't the most skilful display of rugby ever to be seen in the Borders - frequent disagreements about the laws saw to that - but it was a game which had engaged the Border spirit inherited from the days of the reivers.

Nothing could have summed up the approach that was to mark out the character of the Border League better than the first match between Langholm and Hawick in 1873.

There was a lengthy discussion before the match about the laws, most of the argument being over whether a goal should be kicked over the bar or tape, Hawick's favoured option, or under the bar or tape, which Langholm preferred, having inquired into the matter in an earlier fixture with Carlisle.

Langholm won the argument but the game ended in a draw, the ironic point being that Langholm had forced a touchdown, but sent their conversion over the bar.

R. J. Phillips, writing in The Story of Scottish Rugby, took the view that the players, concerning themselves very little about goals, proceeded with the game and found it "a lusty sport admirably suited to the Border temperament".

But it was of course a classic example of the sort of on field incident that was going to liven up Border games for the next century and more.

Langholm, Hawick and Gala were in action against each other 25 years before the new century dawned, and Melrose and Jed-forest or Jedburgh as it was known in the early days, were regular opponents.

Selkirk and Kelso, flitting between junior and senior status, were obviously going to become part of the act, even if they missed out on the first years of the Border Championship as it was originally known.

It now seems likely that the first attempt to bring the Border clubs together developed from the need to pick a representative side to play as the South.

Union Formed to Protect South Interests

It's known that representatives from the South clubs met in 1890 to pick a side to play Edinburgh. There must have been some problems, for another meeting at St Boswells of South rugby men towards the close of the next season was called to discuss some contentious issues.

One of them was "the great dissatisfaction which exists in the South with the present state of matters, and the best way to secure redress of grievances and the furtherance of rugby would be easier promoted through the formation of a South of Scotland Rugby Union".

Thus early was the groundwork laid for the creation of the Border League.

But exactly how the Border clubs organised themselves and created that first competition in 1901-2 is still a mystery. The early minute books disappeared from view years ago, and the first official records of League meetings start only ten years after the first competition.

The early days of rugby in the Borders - Gala at Mossilee around 1900.

The first years of the twentieth century saw the Border championship emerging from the mists in a shape that is still recognisable today, but which was totally lacking in the organisational strength introduced by the League's secretaries and committees over the years.

The results of the early games were listed in league form under the heading of the Border Competition, presumably to avoid confusion with the association football structure of these days which called itself the Border League.

Club records of the first decade of the century are mostly silent on the progress of Border rugby matches, and often even the speakers at the annual general meeting totally ignored their team's success in winning the League over the winter months.

Suggestions that the Scottish Football Union, as it was then known, had frowned on the Border clubs organising competitive rugby have been exaggerated over the years.

But there was probably a reluctance in the Borders, at least in the very earliest years, to upset anyone at headquarters with too dramatic a celebration of local success in a domestic competition which sometimes reached fairly lively conclusions.

However, it's now emerged that the Border clubs made approaches to the Union as early as 1906 for their local competition to be given official blessing.

Grazing at the Melrose Greenyards in the first decade of the League

The Border Championship had been conducted as an irregular sequence of games, and in May of that year Mr J.E. Fairbairn of Melrose made a formal approach to the Union on behalf of the South clubs.

His letter to the Union said that they were making an effort to increase the interest in the rugby game in the District and he went on to ask if the Union's committee would object to the institution of a League for the Borders with a Challenge Cup.

Go Ahead for Formal League

It may have taken considerable discussion, according to the minutes of that historic meeting in May, 1906, but the committee came to the unanimous decision that they should approve the proposed League.

The supportive gentlemen running the Union's affairs then went on to propose that they should subscribe to the Cup, provided they were satisfied with the rules of the proposed League.

Mr Fairbairn was, not surprisingly, back with a copy of the Rules before the start of the new season, and, subject to a few details, they were approved. They are very much the same Rules today, with the addition of such latter-day refinements as bonus points.

The Union, having blessed the League, then went on to underline their support by offering to pay 75 % of the cost of the Cup, provided that it did not exceed £12.

The same cup - the Border Rugby Challenge Cup - is still played for today, but its replacement value is now many hundreds of pounds.

As the Border League minutes of that time no longer appear to exist, there is no formal record of how the Border clubs responded to this gesture from Edinburgh.

But even the best supported of the Border clubs were taking only around £20 a season from gate receipts at this time, and it would be surprising if the Union's gesture had not been well received.

Certainly the local press looked upon the development as good news when it announced that six clubs, Carlisle, Gala, Hawick, Melrose, Langholm and Jedburgh were going to compete together.

The Border Advertiser in September of 1906 declared that "the Border Championship has been put on a more satisfactory basis, and the interest ...... should be much keener than usual.

"The now recognised Championship should have a tendency to elevate the Clubs in the district to a higher standard.

"Six clubs are playing each other, with the exception of Melrose and Langholm, the former not seeing their way to fix with Langholm this season.

"Credit is due to those who have taken the trouble to arrange this competition."

Carlisle, in fact, were never listed in the league tables of 1906-7, even although they had occasional fixtures with the other clubs.

All was now set to go with the newly presented Cup being awarded for the first time at the end of the 1906-7 season to Jed-forest. Now that the relationship with the Union was proceeding smoothly the Riverside club made the most of the occasion.

There have been many stories over the years of the Union's reluctance to recognise the Border League, of photographs of League winning teams being hidden from visiting dignitaries from Edinburgh, and of a general reluctance to tell the story as it was.

But there's enough evidence of leading figures in the game coming to speak at dinners and ground and stand openings in the Borders to suggest that despite the occasional argument relations were pretty good.

The Border League was never inclined to sit back and be lectured at by men from headquarters, as was seen many years later when the Union proposed the introduction of the National Leagues.

And the Borderers occasionally ran into problems with headquarters when they tried to move too quickly. In 1924 the committee had come up with the idea of presenting medals to the Border champions, but received a stony response from Edinburgh.

They sought, and obtained, many reassurances from the Union, notably in 1924 when the Border League committee met to discuss some proposed alterations to the by-laws of the Union.

John Jardine's winning goal kick for Jed-forest against Hawick at Riverside Park in 1913-14

Mr J.A. Smith, down from Edinburgh, calmed some ruffled feathers by emphasising that the objective was to safeguard the senior clubs. And the minutes of that important meeting in April, 1924, quoted Mr Smith as stating "that the Border League would not be interfered with and would carry on as at present".

Recognition of the strength and value of the League - and its importance to Scottish rugby - has been apparent over the years. It did the League no harm either when so many Borderers sat at the top table as President of the Union.

Action was taken in 1932 to avert any threat to the future of the League when a suggestion arose that League games might be played at the end of the season on week nights.

A circular letter to clubs emphasised the position of the League as the bond which had held the Border clubs together and stressed the importance of arranging for all League fixtures to be played on Saturdays.

The National Leagues - and Concern in the Borders

Local concern about the future generally ended with the wholehearted and overwhelming support from member clubs for a continuation of the League, but a new element came into the discussions at the start of the 1970s.

The independence of the Border League as well as its desire to protect the interests of the Border clubs became an issue when the S.R.U. embarked on discussions for the formation of official leagues in Scottish rugby.

The arrival of circulars from Edinburgh immediately raised local anxiety and the League expressed its dissatisfaction with the lack of information on the contentious issues of finance, relegation, management, and other points which the League members could not equate with their own historical position.

Dr George Balfour of Jed-forest was entrusted with the task of representing the views of the seven Border League clubs who, at one point, were prepared "to opt out of the competitive rugby scheme as envisaged by the S.R.U. consultative committee". But they made it clear they would consider an alternative scheme.

The Border clubs, while presenting a united front, had a variety of concerns about the proposals. But underlying their various views was a clear commitment to the continuation of their own historic League.

This stance was maintained as the months dragged on, as compromises were reached, and assurances given. But even after the arrival of competitive rugby at a national level in 1973 the Border clubs were still anxious on several issues.

The clash of representative fixtures with Championship matches exercised them, as did the particularly sensitive communication from headquarters which suggested that Border League fixtures on Saturdays should be cancelled to allow National League fixtures to be played.

This point was raised initially by Hawick who were concerned at a suggestion that their Border League fixture with Gala should be cancelled to allow a National League game with West of Scotland to go ahead.

The importance of the Border clubs sticking together in the face of such proposals became - as was the way of the League - the banner under which the Border case was presented to Edinburgh.

Nearly seventy years had passed since the Union had formally blessed the Border League, but for a short period it looked as though the relationship was under serious strain.

But with compromises, promises, and co-operation, plus some deft work by fixture secretaries, the threat to the long standing harmony was averted.

The fact that the Border clubs, particularly Hawick, made such an impact on the first National leagues did no harm either.

Again, faced with internal concern about the future, the League committee of the late 1970s addressed the question of a possible reshaping of the League.

Too many mid-week games were being arranged for the liking of members and several ideas were floated to reorganise the fixture lists and protect the sevens.

Too Much Rugby Harming League's Health

By the late 1980s, the Border League's concern with the proliferation of games and the impact they were making on the League was undiminished.

Having coped with the problems created by the National competition, the Border League then had to face even more serious complications caused when the Cup, Bowl and Shield knock-out games arrived on the scene.

The League, meeting in 1990, was initially unanimous in condemning any competition which interfered with April Saturdays, and agreed to support it only if it were completed by the end of March.

The sevens, while not formally a matter for the Border League, began to intrude on the League agenda. The Border clubs, driven by their desire to protect the local structure, engaged in lengthy debate and even longer correspondence, in an effort to protect the traditional dates.

Within a few weeks the Union had made it clear that the quarter and semi final games were to be played mid-week, and compromise was in the air. But, faced with the response of other districts in favour of using April Saturdays, the strong line taken by the League was gradually eroded.

The future of Scottish rugby became the buzzword in debate both in the Borders and in the wider Scottish rugby world. The League was awake to the dangers it saw through the dismantling of traditional links, the extra pressure put on players, and a threatened domination from the cities.

Preserving the integrity and historic value of the League was not easy, but the basic principles were never lost sight of.

By the end of the century the club and country issue remained firmly on the League agenda, but support for the national structure has always been inherent, despite some occasional local difficulties, some of which became quite serious.

Fixture lists are now better organised and the problems of the changing game are recognised.

But as it enters its second century the Border League still bears an uncanny resemblance to the shape it bore when it emerged from the first years of uncertainty.

The League still nourishes the links between the Border clubs, enjoys a robust social life, and provides the framework for the game to flourish in the south country — all objectives which the founding fathers would, if they could, applaud today.

The jerseys may have changed a bit over one hundred years, but Melrose and Gala games are still regular fixtures in today's Border League   (Matt Tunnock)

A HUNDRED YEARS IN BORDERS RUGBY

The Border League has never rushed to embrace change, but it has been flexible enough, while guarding its principal objectives of running two rugby competitions, to see that the wider development of the game meant a broad involvement with the Borders rugby scene.

New Faces at the Table

Even although it has set its face against relegation the Border League has always been prepared to consider expanding its numbers, and a fair hearing has been given to those clubs who have wanted to join.

The position of Selkirk and Kelso was clarified fairly quickly when they emerged from their early years. Having moved between senior and junior status virtually from their beginnings, each club was made full members of the League when their results and fixture lists justified it.

Selkirk were admitted in 1908 and Kelso four years later.

But many years were to pass before the League was further enlarged, even although there were occasional attempts by Border clubs to join in.

It was the turn of Earlston in 1923 but a Gala-Hawick combination headed those voting against a proposal for admission which came from Jed-forest and Kelso, and Earlston were rejected by seven votes to four.

From time to time the League looked at other approaches, some of them quite informal, but it took until 1996 for the next enlargement, when Peebles were invited to join in.

A Helping Hand

Over the century the Border League, while never itself awash with cash, has helped out both senior and junior clubs, has given to rugby charities and others with a wider appeal, and has managed its financial affairs with a proper regard for its two principal aims, the running of the Border League competition and the Border District Championship.

The very special difficulties which faced Langholm in the first part of the century occasionally surfaced on the League's agenda. The League committee was conscious of the geographical problems which faced the Dumfriesshire club, and went out of their way to help where they could.

In 1928 Langholm were given £10 to help with the repair of the bridge into their ground, a sum which seems ridiculous today, but which represented around 50 per cent of the League's annual income at that time.

This investment in the future of the game in the furthest corner of the League's territory was not the only help given, and assistance with special fund raising games was often provided.

Semi juniors, juniors and schools were all helped by the League over the years, and the only bleak note as far as generosity was concerned can be found in 1914.

On the outbreak of war, with rugby being suspended, it was decided that the League should make no donation to the War funds. But as the League's funds had risen to only £20 by the time the war was over the caution of the committee is probably understandable.

Welcome to the Visitors

One of the major events of the 1920s was the visit of the touring New South Wales team.

The financing of the hospitality which was extended to them exercised the Border League at many meetings, not surprisingly with the expenses amounting to just over £87.

But for that sum there were tours of the four Abbeys at Melrose, Dryburgh, Kelso and Jedburgh, and a run out to St Mary's Loch and the Devil's Beef Tub.

It's not only the overall costs which seems so strange today - it's doubtful if a touring side in the twenty first century would welcome the same itinerary.

Paying off the bills for this pilgrimage was eventually settled by a levy of £10 on each of the Border clubs, and a number of Hawick gentlemen offered to donate £12 to bring the books into order.

With a further donation of £3 from Hawick, and an additional levy of £1. 10 shillings all round, the League's debts were honourably cleared.

The Rougher Side of Rugby

Border League rugby has never been short of the competitive spirit, and there have been some pretty robust encounters over the hundreds of games last century.

But, bearing in mind the intensity of local competition, comparatively few players have been sent off, and there's always been a sense that a fairly direct approach to the game was in the best spirit of the Borders.

Just occasionally things have got out of hand and Gala must have felt that stage was reached in a match against Kelso in 1931.

The Netherdale side lodged a complaint with the League about rough play alleged to have happened in the game.

The Kelso representatives rejected the allegation but gave the committee an assurance that Kelso would do everything in their power to prevent the possibility of such a thing happening.

In the spirit of harmony that generally surfaced when such allegations came up, Gala accepted the assurance. But the League, feeling that there was a tendency towards rough play, wrote to all the clubs to stamp it out.

It was felt that a certain type of spectator was indirectly responsible for the encouragement of unseemly conduct, including bad language, and club officials were urged to ban such undesirables from their grounds.

Players on the Move

As the century ended there was much talk in Border circles of transfers, of alleged poaching of players, of the end of the club loyalty which had marked a hundred years of competition.

But in fact players had been moving pretty freely between the Border clubs since before the League was formally set up.

The reasons were very similar to those given today, although cash and cars were of course never mentioned.

But desire to play in a better class of rugby or to make a bid for a Scottish cap, together with moves which followed better job prospects, all contributed to a fairly big shift in playing personnel.

Some players, such as Wattie Forrest of Kelso, moved to Hawick before being capped for Scotland. He returned to Kelso eventually but only to play association football.

Another Kelso player of the first decade of the century, Carl Ogilvy, had equally itchy feet, and moved to Melrose for a season before going over to Hawick where he too was capped. Kelso, of course, had not permanently secured senior status, and the wish to play in a higher grade of rugby was understandable. The same arguments apply today.

Even earlier, before the League was conceived, Tom Scott, who got his first cap at Melrose, moved to Hawick to build up his international career.

Scores of players over the years have sought to change clubs, and a regular feature of Border League meetings was the item when applications to move were tabled, mostly from junior players.

The committee on the whole was generally understanding, but there have been many cases where applications have been turned down. And at senior level there have been cases too where no permission was forthcoming, the League resisting wherever possible the chances of a player appearing in the same season for two League clubs.

Rugby in the Schools

The League has for many years regarded the development of future players in the Borders as being of direct relevance to its main objects, the running of the League and District championship.

To meet this concern a schools liaison sub committee, led for a lengthy period by Tom Purves of Gala, sought, through regular meetings with the education authority, to maintain rugby as the principal sport in the Border schools.

The age old problem of clashes between school fixtures and semi junior rugby, the supply of rugby teachers in schools, and the vital importance of continued links between schools and clubs were the recurring issues.

The League, over the years, helped the Schools Association financially and the century ended with friendly and co-operative liaison between the clubs and the schools.

Train Times

The Border teams depended heavily on the trains which ploughed through the main and branch lines until their final sad disappearance. Not only was there an invaluable regular service which influenced kick-off times, but special trains were laid on for many years, carrying hundreds of supporters to the games which dominated Border sporting life.

But as is the way of train travel, the service was not always to be relied upon.

One journalist, writing in The Border Advertiser in 1904, obviously had hoped for better things than the joys of rail travel on a Saturday afternoon.

"The Gala team, along with a number of their enthusiastic supporters, left Galashiels Station on Saturday en route for "Jethart - the Justice City", a distance of about 22 miles, at 25 minutes past 3.

"After a weary wait at St Boswells, changing at 2 junctions, and a 'processional ride' between small stations, the train steamed into Jedburgh at exactly a quarter past five - thereby completing the journey in 1 hour 50 minutes, or behind time by 41 minutes."

Life was complicated in those days, and the game, which didn't start until 6.25 p.m., and which had an abbreviated first half, ran into major problems with the light, or lack of it.

The referee decided that the second half should last only as long as the light...and then there was presumably the train journey back to Gala to look forward to.

Langholm were specially vulnerable to train problems, and had the added expense of having to send a telegram to the Carlisle stationmaster asking him to have the Carlisle/Edinburgh train stop at Riddings Junction to pick up the team.

The Langholm secretary was taken to task for sending needlessly lengthy and expensive telegrams, and the following Saturday the train roared past the waiting players.

It was found that the economical telegram sent on that occasion read simply "Stop train - Wull".

 # GALA

SUCCESSES - AND NEAR MISSES

For a team which was one of the first Border sides to join the Scottish Rugby Union, which has been celebrated the length of the land for its prowess in sevens, which has won three official championships as well as one in the long gone days of the unofficial or "newspaper" championship, Gala have been strangely quiet in the domestic world of the Border League.

Only six times have Gala won the league outright, a thin enough return for their hundred years of competition. And one of them, in 1905-6, even denied them the cup, it not being presented until the following year.

Gala's failure to deliver the title more often surely rests in the Maroons' notorious habit of going off the boil when things are getting interesting.

They have seldom been a team which went on the rampage against weak opponents, and despite some big scoring in the 1970s, they've often seemed reluctant to ram home their superiority.

The four big years of Gala's history, when they won the unofficial championship in 1931-2, and the official one in three seasons in the early eighties, only twice produced the double of the Border League cup to go alongside the Scottish title.

Fixture Mix-up Ruins Gala's Chances

Gala nearly pulled off their first win in the new championship as early as 1904. By the end of January the only blemish on their record was a draw with Jed-forest, who were pressing hard for the top spot.

Gala looked very much like finishing as the leading Border club until they met Langholm and lost to a splendid drop goal from near the touch line at midfield by Langholm's internationalist Tom Scott.

The irony of this was that the game was only fixed up when Edinburgh Wanderers couldn't fulfil their due fixture at Mossilee.

Langholm, who weren't even on the Gala card at the beginning of the season, filled in, defeated the Maroons, and opened the door to Jedforest.

This sort of irregular fixture list was one of the reasons why the Border clubs decided to make their approach to the Union to have the competition formally recognised.

The following week a disputed try near the end at Riverside, with a special train having brought the Gala supporters over, was virtually the decider for the Border championship.

Middlemiss scored the only try of the game for Jed in the closing minutes and it was reported "that it was regrettable, as the ball was alleged to be out of play. The Jed touch judge was consulted, and the try awarded. A draw would have been a more accurate verdict."   So said the match report, but, in the best traditions of the Border game, little more was made of what was, at the time, a controversial incident.

Gala's first success in the League came in only the fifth season of the competition, 1905-6.   Here was early promise from the Maroons, but the League was still in its youthful days and Kelso and Selkirk were yet to join in.

Gala had eight games to play that year, winning five and drawing three, including both the matches against Hawick.

But there must have been something very positive about the Gala defence in 1905-6, with only five points being recorded against them. They came from Langholm in the fixture on the windy heights of Mossilee, Gala getting home by 6-5.

G.S.Scott was the captain of that victorious team which included, among other notables, Willie McCrirrick, who was at the height of his fame as a scrum half - the first of a long line of notable players who have since occupied that position in the Gala team.

It took until 1921-2 for Gala to come back to the top, after a war that had taken heavy toll of rugby players in the Borders.

Half Backs Show Gala the Way

Gala were pursuing the erratic course that marked so much of their play over the years, but despite losing games to the city clubs they had a much needed triumph in the League.

They were a well balanced outfit, with lots of pace and style. The flying Andrew Murdison played on the wing, and Tom Waddell was the steadiest of full backs.

League Champions Gala in 1921-2
Back Row - W. Aitchison (Groundsman), W. Purves, J. McRae, J. Beattie, D. Roy,
  W. E. Kyle (Referee), C. F. Brown, D. Crearar, A. Walker, M. Flynn,
  A. Polson (Touch Judge)
Middle row - J. Lumsden, T. Waddell, A. Murdison, D. W. Cockburn (Capt), G. R. Turner,
  W. R. Ovens
Front Row - A. O. Wishart, J. Millar

The half back partnership of Alex Wishart and George Turner (although the latter sometimes turned out at centre) was one of many effective pairings produced by Gala this century.

Among the forwards were Jock Beattie, Charlie (Chay) Brown, Duncan Roy and the captain Dave Cockburn.

In those days clubs went to the greatest of lengths to make sure that whenever possible games were played in the most inclement of winters. On one famous occasion it is on record that braziers were lit and burned all night at Netherdale to thaw out the pitch and to allow the match with Hawick to go on the next day.

Perhaps because of the commitment most matches in these days were hotly contested affairs where a score of any sort was a major event.

So when Gala won by 24 - 5 points in a crucial game against Kelso the five tries were regarded at Netherdale with great enthusiasm.

It was their biggest score since before the war, and set the team up for only their second league triumph.

That Gala supporters were going to have to wait another 28 years, and endure another world war before their next success would scarcely have seemed credible.

And when the next success came it was only half a triumph. In 1949-50 the title was shared with Melrose. Gala won nine of their games, losing only to Hawick and Langholm in two vital consecutive games as the season neared its end.....another example of the Maroons letting an opportunity slip by.

But for an unaccountable lapse in February the Maroons, who were captained by Jackie (Shacks) Murray, would have been undisputed Border Champions. They had made a great start to the competition, winning their first eight matches. Their ninth match, against Melrose at Netherdale,was postponed because of frost.

Typical Border League forwards of the 1950s - Bob Wilson and Tom Elliot of Gala

In their tenth they met Hawick at Netherdale and suffered their first League defeat. Even worse for the Maroons' large following was to follow, for on the very next Saturday they went to Milntown Park and were beaten by Langholm.

Their win in the last League game with Kelso brought the Braw Lads level with Melrose and it was necessary to play off the game cancelled in January.

The crucial last match was against Melrose at Netherdale on a midweek April evening, and with both sides desperate for the win that would secure the title it ended in a 6-6 draw.

Gala's points, from George Burrell's drop and Bob Wilson's penalty, gave them a share of the League championship, but the season was wearing on too quickly for a decider to be fixed up.

Some Gala folk thought that their earlier win at the Greenyards in September gave them a moral claim to the title, but it was a bid made more in hope than with serious expectation, and a general agreement to share the 1949-50 title was the obvious solution.

The years rolled on, and it was 1966-7 before the next Netherdale triumph.

John Gray was captain, and having run up 115 points without reply in their opening three games against city sides, Gala embarked on their League bid in fine fettle.

Tight Defence Sees Gala Through

Their defence was virtually try proof, and they conceded only nine points in their first four League games. After handing out Melrose's biggest defeat in nine years Gala went on to beat Hawick before running into a stream of injuries, the most serious being the one that saw Duncan Paterson sidelined.

The title bid was really sown up early in the second half of the season, with only a draw against Melrose to mar the run, and the second last game against Kelso saw Jock Turner kick Gala home.

John Gray accepted the cup at Poynder Park after an incident packed game when Kelso scored the only try of the afternoon.

When it was all over Gala conceded 28 points to Hawick in their last league match, but the Cup was safely in the Netherdale display case by that time.

Selkirk, who had lost narrowly at Netherdale, never got the chance to play the return fixture, but Gala had won, easing up, in what was to be their last victory for another 13 years.

League Champions Gala in 1966-7
L. to R. Back Row-G. L. Houghton, D. Hardie, I. W. K. Crosbie, P. B. Townsend,
J. M. Russell, R. M. Paterson, D. G. Brydon, W. K. Brydon.
L. to R. Centre Row-A. D. Gill, A. A. Carson, L. B. Rodger, G. K. Oliver,
J. S. Wilkinson, R. D. Murray, N. Polson, T. Campbell, J. H. Dobson.
L. to R. Front Row-M. C. Brunton, T. P. Carruthers (Hon. Match Secretary),
D. S. Paterson (Vice-Captain), J. L. Turner (President), John Gray (Captain),
J. S. Mitchell (Hon. Secretary), J. W. C. Turner, T. S. F. Veitch (Hon. Treasurer),
T. Jack. Absent-H. L. Dobson, D. G. Napier.

When success did come again, in 1979-80 and again the following year, it was particularly sweet for the Netherdale faithful. It broke into what turned out to be a run of 12 Hawick victories.

The first year of the double came with Jim Aitken as captain. Gala reversed their usual trend and made a slow start to this League success with a 3-3 draw at Philiphaugh, and looked far from championship material.

But they had two outstanding kickers in Peter Dods and Arthur Brown, and two pacy wingers in Don Ledingham and Vic (Chipper) Chlebowski, who scored 40 tries between them in all games in the course of the season.

Pickings weren't so rich in the Border League, but even so Gala still turned in scores of 51-0 against Jed-forest and 31-0 when facing Melrose.

Gala's notorious inconsistency tag was shed next year, when they held on to the League title, again with Jim Aitken as captain.

It was Selkirk again who looked like upsetting things in an early game, but by the time the League programme was building up after the New Year Gala were on a roll and dropped only a point to Kelso.

Their double over Hawick was the first since 1952-3 and was widely accepted as a vital element in the Gala success.

Another Gray, Another Title

It took the arrival in 1997-8 of John Gray's son Richie as captain to bring another League title to Netherdale.

There's certainly something in the like father, like son, tag. Gala won the Melrose sevens in 1932 with Henry Polson in the side, their first success at The Greenyards tournament since his father played in the 1903 seven.

By now the expanded Border League meant that 14 games were on the card, and Gala played all of them in their sixth outright success.

By earlier standards this was a year of phenomenally high scoring, no fewer than 403 points coming from the 14 League games.

The season had the brightest of starts with convincing wins over Hawick and Melrose, but the calls of the Premiership and the Scottish Cup meant that Gala played only two Border League games in their first 11 matches.

By the time the season had turned the Maroons were scoring at more than 20 points in each League game, and with Gary Parker leading the goal kicking they were out in front before the first defeat, Hawick winning the return game at Mansfield.

The only two blemishes were away defeats at Mansfield and Poynder Parks and there was a bit of a fright when playing Kelso. Gala wrapped up the season with an eight try burst against Langholm, which clinched the title on a ground which had often enough proved disastrous in the past.

Since then Gala have threatened, have often led the table, have produced some dramatic victories against the forecasts, but have yet to add to their six outright wins in the whole century of competitive Border rugby.

The Big Match

The Game That Inspired a Song

There might be different ideas in other clubrooms, but at Mansfield Park and Netherdale the feeling would be that to sum up the Border League and all it has stood for over a hundred years, you need only call upon any one of scores of Gala - Hawick games.

Hawick may have won the bulk of the series, but there was a special quality about so many of the matches that they came to typify the entire Border League.

So it was in February, 1981, when Gala took a major step towards the Border League and Division I championship in one of Mansfield Park's most thrilling encounters.

Not many games give birth to a song, but Henry Douglas's lament for a match lost all because of referee Alan Hosie's watch still gets an airing in Border rugby circles - but not often in Gala.

It had always been an enthralling afternoon, with the biggest crowd of the season watching some power play matched to a splendid display of running rugby.

Gala v. Hawick at Netherdale in 1982-3 with Jock Berthinussen, Derek White and Ian Easson prominent for Gala, Colin Deans with the ball and Alan Tomes coming in to help. (Border Telegraph)

The two full backs, Peter Dods and John Hogg, were outstanding, and the fact that the game's three tries came from the Hawick wingers Taylor and Mitchell, and Gala's from Dods, said much about the desire of both teams to keep the game open.

It was a drop goal from Arthur Brown in five minutes that gave Gala the perfect start, but after a series of missed penalty goals, Jim Renwick created the first try. Hogg missed the conversion, but a one point lead was the marker for a gripping second half. (These were the days of the four point try).

A penalty from Brown put Gala in front again, but just as time was running out, Hawick's second try followed an inspired piece of running by Hogg.

The tension was acute as Renwick missed the conversion, but it was into injury time and Alan Hosie was noted to be looking closely at the famous watch.

At 8-6 for Hawick the home side were, if not in command, at least prepared to sit out the final seconds.

But Dods raced into the attack, shrugging off several tackles. With support beside him Hawick waited for the pass, and waited again. But Dods had seen a gap, accelerated through and went in at the left hand corner for a try that broke a few Hawick hearts.

Gala went on to win the Border League and the Division 1 championship, but they had no more close calls, and after the Mansfield Park thriller few would have wanted them. And no more songs were written that season at least.

Jed's Sixteen Men

One of best stories coming out of the Jed-forest annals concerns the day in the 1930s when the Riverside men travelled to Philiphaugh in their usual coach. But one player, who happened to possess a private car, travelled to Selkirk on his own.

Arriving first he changed into his kit and went off for some light jogging. He took refuge from a heavy shower, and arrived back at the ground to see the game started. Jed had filled his missing place with their trainer on the assumption that the car had broken down.

Unnoticed, he nipped on to the field and Jed enjoyed the luxury of an extra man until near the interval when Belle Murray, a staunch Selkirk supporter, shouted out "Coont the players, ref !" A swift check and Jed started the second period with the right number.

Nowadays, with replacements flooding on to the field in most matches, will it be long before another 16 man team appears ?

 # HAWICK

THE GREEN MACHINE ROLLS ON

When Neil Stenhouse's goal kicks saw Hawick through to victory in the final Border League match of the first hundred years he was ensuring that the Greens were finishing as they had started.

Hawick, as they were to do with the first official championship and with the first Scottish Cup, had long ago won the first Border competition in the first season of last century.

In between times of course they had secured their place as the outstanding Border side, winning the League on no fewer than 42 occasions, and sharing it with Jed-forest on one occasion before the first World War.

Hawick's superiority over the other Border clubs has been as marked in the League as in other areas of the Scottish rugby scene.

Dominant for long periods in sevens, winners of both the unofficial championship and, even more positively in the early years of the National League, their success came in surges which left the other Border sides floundering in their wake.

But, as in most of the other Border textile towns, extraneous influences affected the play of the Hawick rugby club over the years.

The lead up years to the formation of the first Border league were not kind to Hawick. Many families left the town as the hosiery industry declined in the 1890s, and Hawick was always a target for the scouts from the Northern Union game.

But, with the coming of the first organised Border competition Hawick lifted their game and were installed as winners. The crucial match was in Galashiels, and Walter Forrest who had moved from Kelso to get senior experience with Hawick, dropped a goal for a 4-0 win.

That was a vital score, as Gala had the edge on Hawick with a win in the first and a draw in the second of two earlier matches, including the game at Mansfield Park.

It was common in the early years of competition on the Border circuit for three games to be played, two of them as competitive games and the third (which was not always the last of the three) being regarded as a friendly to be called upon for League points only if the weather interfered with either of the others.

That early Hawick side was captained by Bill Kyle, who went on to play for Scotland, and who was regarded as one of the outstanding forwards of his time, being not only a fine dribbler, but a great catcher of the ball.

First Of Many Cups for Hawick

It took Hawick a few years to get back into their stride in the Borders as first Jed-forest and then Gala took the honours.

But they got their hands on the recently presented cup for the first time in 1908-9 when they also shared the unofficial championship with Watsonians.

Bill Kyle was still playing, but under the captaincy of Sandy Burns Hawick had emerged as a power in the land. They won all their matches in the League, but had to share it with Jed-forest the following year.

This was one of only two occasions when the League honours were tied, although of course there were others when sheer pressure of fixtures led to the competition being declared void.

Rugby was serious stuff around that time, and Mansfield Park, according to a report of the time, staged what amounted to a minor riot during a Hawick-Gala game.

The referee had been far from popular, and the crowds invaded the field. "A scene of great disorder prevailed, missiles being thrown at the official and the county police had to intervene, as did some of the Hawick players and officials."

A short ban was opposed on Hawick playing within ten miles of their home ground for the rest of the month.

Matches in the League continued at this very intense level with the competition arousing great local passions. The winning Hawick sequence could only be broken by a play-off, and 1910-11 saw the decider at Riverside Park ending with Hawick losing to Melrose.

But, with five internationalists in the side - Bill Kyle, Walter Sutherland, Robert Lindsay-Watson, Billy Burnet and another ex-Kelso man Carl Ogilvy, Hawick took command in the years leading to the war.

Border League Champions 1913-14 *Back row*: P.Hope (trainer), J.T.Michie, A.O.Robson, J.R.Morgan, W.G.Anderson, G.Johnstone, J.Corrie*, G.W.T.Laing, J.Helm, A.Burns (team committee). *Middle*: J.Glendinning (secretary), W.Ker*, D.T.Gass, W.R.Sutherland*, Dr J.Oliver Hamilton (president), W.Burnet (captain), T.Wilson*, D.Fiddes. *Front*: J.Docherty, F.Beatson, J.Charters*, A.P.Turnbull.
(The players marked with an asterisk were killed in the Great War. James Michie, Frank Beatson and David Fiddes were wounded).

One of their triumphs came in the last year before the break, but, like the rest of the Border towns, Hawick sent many of its finest to the front, and league rugby closed down.

It did not take long for the Greens to get back into the leading position after the break.

They defeated Jed-forest at Melrose in a play-off in 1920-1, anticipating the situation in the final season of the century.

The Train Whistle Sounds for Hawick

The big difference was that in 1920-1 the Border League secretary had been instructed to write to the Railway Company for special trains to be laid on from Kelso, Jedburgh, Hawick, Galashiels and Selkirk.

With support as enthusiastic as at any time in their history, Hawick embarked on a tremendous run throughout the 1920s.

They won eight of the Border League titles, including a play-off against Kelso at Melrose.

More great names were emerging. Willie Welsh and Jerry Foster, two of the club's renowned international forwards, first played in 1925-6.

Captained by George "Dod" Cairns the following year, Hawick won the League again, as was beginning to be inevitable, and topped it with the Scottish championship and a grand slam of the five Border spring sevens tournaments.

Willie Mactaggart and Rob Storrie were two of the outstanding threequarter line, and a pair of the club's most memorable half backs, Cameron Keillor and Willie Corbett made a tremendous impact.

Great teams - and this was certainly one of Hawick's best - leave a big gap behind them when they break up, and Hawick certainly suffered during the 1930s. One Border League triumph at the start of the decade was followed by a share in the Scottish championship, but they were thin years for the Mansfield faithful.

The calls of the Rugby League clubs in England would not be denied, and first Willie Welsh and then Alec Fiddes left the town. When the second World War interrupted rugby like so much else, Hawick was far from being at its peak.

A general levelling out in the game, plus the influence of some severe weather, led the post war years to becoming much more even. With Gala, Melrose, Hawick and Selkirk all taking a share of the honours at home, no clear pattern for success was emerging.

But gradually Hawick began to stretch clear of the field as they had done in the 1920s. Rugby, like much else, was booming with the economy recovering, and there were plenty stars around the Border scene to hold the attention of the large crowds.

The first clear signs of Hawick's recovery came in 1954-5 and the following season, both of them years of Border League success.

A back division that included Norman Davidson, a classic stand-off, the colourful and unpredictable George Stevenson, the powerful running of Wattie Scott, and the craft of scrum half Jackie Wright, was always going to be a match and more than that for any team.

With the total control exerted up front by international forwards such as Hugh McLeod, Jack Hegarty and Adam Robson it was no surprise to find Hawick embarking on a run of Border success that brought them 19 Cups out of the 25 competitions up to 1979-80.

Hawick's Finest ?

It was claimed by many that Jack Hegarty's team of 1959-60 was the pick of the bunch.

With Oliver Grant and Ronnie Grieve contributing to the forward strength, and the celebrated half back pairing of Drew Broatch and Glen Turnbull, Hawick won the League with a clean sweep over the best the Border clubs could offer.

Hawick Border and Scottish Champions 1959-60.
Back row: E.W.Broatch, T.S.Barker, R.Valentine, T.O.Grant, D.Murray, J.Cunningham, B.King, A.R.Broatch. Middle: R.J.Grieve, J.Wallace, A.Robson, G.D.Stevenson, W.J.Hunter, R.B.Brydon, C.Renwick, T.Edmison, D.Grant. Front row: W.D.Jackson, J.H.Gray, H.F.McLeod, J.J.Hegarty (captain), T.Wright (president), I.Fraser, A.Renwick, G.H.Willison, R.G.Turnbull.

More calls from the Rugby League, including those to Broatch and Turnbull, as well as to Rob Valentine, meant a rebuilding, but the Greens made shrewd replacements and continued to dominate the Border scene.

New names crowded on to the Mansfield Park scene - Jim Renwick and Alastair Cranston teaming up in the centre, and Norman Pender and Ian Barnes making a powerful impact on opposition packs.

With eight straight wins in a row, and a span of 21 triumphs in the 26 seasons from 1959-60 to 1984-5, Hawick stretched their dominance of the Border League.

It was said that Hawick were rebuilding at the start of the eighties, but with Colin Deans and Jim Renwick making a powerful impact they had the nucleus of another fine team.

Hawick were not as powerful up front as in seasons gone by, and began to rely more on their ability to make heavier packs work harder to stay in touch. The ball flowed around the field, the goal kicking of Colin Gass brought points galore, and the four Border League wins which followed Gala's double between 1979 and 1981 were richly enjoyed.

The combination of retirals, injuries, the restructuring of the game both in laws and fixtures, made Hawick's task of staying at the top in the nineties a lot harder - and the emergence of Melrose as the dominant team in the Borders produced some classic games at Mansfield and The Greenyards.

League successes in 1988-9 and 1995-6 were all that the Greens could secure - thin pickings by their own high standards.

But as the first hundred years of the Borders' own very personal competition came to an end Hawick finished as they had started.

Late Finish Sees Hawick Home

The longest ever season saw Hawick and Selkirk engaged in the playing of two postponed games, Hawick winning both and picking up the bonus points that ensured a play-off, with Jed-forest providing the opposition.

Not played until May 18th, the match was the latest ever finish to the Border League, and reflected great credit on all who ensured that the hundredth year ended on the most positive of notes.

While not a classic, it was a great contest between the two Border teams who had dominated the first years of the League and who were still there at the finish.

Hawick produced one of their traditional late recoveries to overtake Jed-forest's interval lead, and Neil Stenhouse's second half goals brought them their 43rd Border League title.

That one team should have so dominated the competition throughout the first hundred years could be looked upon as creating the ultimate in frustration for the less successful.

But the quality of Hawick's play has set a standard for Scottish domestic rugby that, under the new structure of the game, is scarcely likely to be matched by any other club.

League Champions Hawick in 1999-2000

Back Row - A. Lang, A. Marsh, G. McLeod, A. Stevenson, W. Davies, A. Imray,
  G. Walker, R. Deans, G. Murdie, A. Gillie
Middle row - G. Douglas, C. Rodgerson, K. Scott, N. Douglas, E, Butler, G. Sharp,
  I. Elliot, D. Murphy, S. McLeod, A. Gray, C. Turnbull, B. Keown, K. Moffat,
  R. Philbin, K. Davidson
Front Row - N. Stenhouse, D. Hughes, C. Murray, S. Welsh (Capt), R. Bell (President),
  K. Reid, A. Takarangi, J. McDevitt

(Photograph Jim Rowan Hawick)

The Big Match

Jim Renwick Ends Gala Hopes

When a Gala-Hawick game gets to the fourth minute of injury time, stand back for fireworks.

Once again the seconds were being counted off when the winning score came in yet another Gala-Hawick game, the match that virtually decided both the Border League and the Division 1 championship in February, 1982.

Hawick's triumph was a particularly sweet one for the Greens. Not only did it occur on the Gala ground, but it set them up for the Border League and the Division I title, ending the Maroons' chance of a third successive Scottish title.

There was a great clutch of internationalists, past, present and future, around Netherdale that February afternoon. Peter Dods was at full back, with Jim Aitken, Bobby Cunningham, Tom Smith, Derek White and Gordon Dickson in the Gala pack. And Hawick matched them with Jim Renwick, Keith Murray, Alastair Cranston, Colin Deans, Alan Tomes, Derek Turnbull and Alastair Campbell in green jerseys.

With names like that around it wasn't in the least surprising to find that the old photographs show a big crowd deep around the ropes.

The game lived up to its billing - but Gala can still look back on it as a great chance lost. Even if Hawick did miss four penalties, Gala missed six, some of them easy.

Dods had a first half penalty to set against Hawick's drop and penalty from Colin Gass, not long gone from Gala to play for Hawick, and a Renwick penalty.

Gala got the only try, Jim Maitland collecting at midfield, gathering his own high kick and beating Colin Gass for a score which Dods would normally have expected to convert but which on this occasion slid by.

Hawick's Jim Renwick waits while Gala's Vic Chlebowski is in the action at Netherdale in 1982   (Border Telegraph)

The excitement built up as Gala piled on the pressure and Tom Smith went over from a maul under the Hawick posts, but referee Brian Anderson fetched him back for offside.

Into injury time, a Maitland drop goal, and the Gala fans were ecstatic, but there was still the sting in the tail that so often added the flavour to Gala-Hawick matches.

Renwick set up a ruck 40 yards out from the posts, Gala killed the ball, and the Hawick skipper had a decision to make. In his own words "I looked over to Colin Gass, or to anyone else who fancied the kick, to take it. In the end, I just took it myself. I just thought, keep your head down and hit it."

This he duly did, the ball went over, the final whistle went, and there was jubilation in the Hawick camp.

And there was no Gala Henry Douglas to write a lament about Brian Anderson's watch.

Fast Scoring in Early Days

What is thought to be the quickest try - and one of the most unusual - ever scored in the Border League came in the opening seconds of a Melrose-Hawick game in 1907.

Charlie Gillie kicked off for Melrose, ballooned the ball, and Adam Hope, following up hard, caught it in the air and burst through the opposing forwards.

He handed it on to J.J. Fairbairn who went through the rest of the Hawick team to score between the posts, the ball never having touched the ground or one of the opposing players.

The Border Rugby Guide, which was created by the late John Robertson, for many years the secretary and treasurer of the League, was continued after his death as a memorial to his work for Borders rugby.

Links between the Border Schools Rugby Union and the League have been strong and the League makes regular donations to the funds of the Union.

JED-FOREST

SUCCESSFUL EARLY YEARS

Few teams have made such an impact on a new competition as Jed-forest did in the early days of organised Border rugby.

League Champions Jed-forest in 1906-7
Back Row: R. Wight (inset), G. Stewart (Secretary), Ex-Provost Laidlaw (President), R. Douglas, W. Purdie (Match Committee), A. Veitch (inset).
Second Row: A Renilson, W L Huggan, J. B. Wilson, W Balfour, M Drummond, W. Fish, J. T. Robson, C. W Stewart, W. B. Jardine.
Front Row: R. Aitken, W Hall, G.M. Oliver (Captain), R. Lunn (Vice-Captain), J. S. Waugh, W. Purdie.

After letting Hawick have first shot at the title, the Royal Blues (who might have been known still as the Chocolate and Whites, if they hadn't abandoned their experimental strip of the 1890s) then won the League in five of the next six seasons, starting in 1902-3.

They were mostly clean cut wins in the early days, but one of the successes came after a play-off.

When the Border League cup was presented for the first time it was only appropriate that Jed-forest should collect it. They had clearly taken over from Hawick as the leading side in the Borders.

And Jed went on to make a proper job of it too, winning the unofficial championship the same year, 1906-7.

After the last match of the season against Watsonians a dinner was hosted by George Crabbie, who was vice president of Jed-forest that year. The Border League cup was handed over by Adam Turnbull of Hawick, the League president.

In the best traditions of Borders rugby he declared that the cup had been won by the best team, one in which their was not a weak spot, and a team which was a fine example for every team in the Borders.

The 1907-8 season marked the appearance of tangible rewards to the players. Jed-forest having won the Border Championship Cup for the second time the committee decided to present them with gold badges as a token of the good work they had done at the Melrose play-off.

Some of the players who stepped forward were William Hall, William B. Jardine, Michael Drummond, J.S. Waugh, William C. Balfour, William Watson, J.T. Robson, G. M.Oliver, Adam Renilson and William Purdie.

Jed-forest then went on to tie with Hawick in 1909-10 but no decider could be fixed up.

Like most Border teams Jed-forest has carried a roll-call of local names down the years. Some of them, such as the team captains Michael

Drummond, William Purdie, James V. Henderson, W.C. Balfour, and William Laidlaw, all from the early years of the century, have featured in Riverside team sheets for years.

Back from the War to Win Again

After the excitement of the opening years of the League Jed-forest fell back and it was not until the first World War had come and gone that they again took the title, in the first year after the resumption of rugby, 1919-20.

The league title, which was again accompanied by the Scottish unofficial championship, was won with a 100% record. Eleven games were played, the only one outstanding being the return game against Melrose, which the Greenyards side turned down on the basis that the title had already been won.

Captain in that historic year was Willie Scott, and he led his side to set up the proud undefeated record which stood until it was surpassed by Hawick in 1960.

Long years were to come and go, and another world war to intervene, before the League title came back to Riverside Park.

But before the celebrations of 1956-7, there was a strong claim from Riverside, and from Poynder Park and the Greenyards, for another League success.

The 1947-48 title chase had run into weather problems and was running late.

Kelso were the team of the year, and had won the unofficial championship, while being doggedly pursued in the Borders by Jed-forest and Melrose.

Weather Denies Three Teams

On the last day of March torrential rain and the strongest of winds hit Riverside when Kelso and Jed-forest met in a match that ended in a win for the Foresters by two Charlie McDonald penalties to one from Archie Ferguson.

The three teams, Jed, Kelso and Melrose, all ended with identical records of played 12, won seven, lost three and drawn two.

The League committee, even when faced with the prospect of April and the sevens being upon them, looked seriously at the possibility of calling for the clubs to fix up play-off games. But eventually they accepted the reality of the situation and settled for a void championship.

Even after more than 50 years there is still a feeling in three Border clubs that one of the most exciting of seasons might have been resolved with credit going to someone.

All three teams involved still look back on the year of 1947-8 as one in which they shared the Border League championship.

Indeed, the official Jed history says that for the first time in 27 years Jed had attained Border League honours. It must have been hard for the late Iain Mackenzie, editor of the history, to have to record the Border League Committee's decision that the championship was void.

Jed's Great Scottish Names

There were some great names in the Jed side around that time. Charlie McDonald and David Rose were both Scottish internationalists, with McDonald desperately unlucky to gain but one cap. Their presence in the Jed sides of the these days added colour and style to the many Border League games in which they appeared.

Jed-forest shared the unofficial championship in 1956-7, and once again added the Border title to their honours.

They had started the season with a tour in Cornwall, picked up the Selkirk sevens cup in September, and then embarked on what was to be a highly successful season.

Despite a run of injuries to Douglas "Baldy" Lightbody, Wilson Renilson, Harry Hogg, and Bert Hunter, Jed kept on track and recorded a memorable double over Hawick. The fact that the Greens couldn't manage a single score in either game said much for the Jed defence.

The big night in the Jed season followed the return game at Mansfield. After their win the Foresters returned home in triumph, their bus was piped into the town, with skipper Baldy Lightbody holding the Border League cup, and Provost Elliot gave them a civic welcome.

It was said that the celebrations had all been planned before Jed had even set out for Hawick. That was a measure of the confidence and pride that marked out that Jed-forest side as one of the outstanding of the century.

The one minor blot on the season came from the final accounts, which showed a loss of £3. 13. 6d but since the Cornish tour at the start of the year accounted for more expenditure than the entire season's drawings at the gate, perhaps it wasn't such a bad set of figures after all.

League Champions Jed-forest in 1956-7
Back Row: W. Lunn, R. Nimmo, G. Balfour, G. Redpath, W Brown, W Tait, A. Elliot
Third Row: J. Wilson, W Jackson, G. Bunyan, P. Cuthbertson, F Hawkins, R. Notman, H. Younger, R. Hunter G. Lyall, G. Miller J. Brodie, F. Rose.
Second Row: G. McDonald, A. Bell, W. Dodds, C. Renilson, D. Lightbody, J. R. B. Wilson (President), R. Veitch, G. Forbes, W. Hume, L Middlemiss, J. McDowell.
Front Row: W. Rose, L Henderson, G. Renilson, G. Mitchell.

And the Border League statistics were pretty good too, with only one defeat in the 12 games played.

The following year saw the start of another barren period for the club, as far as Border honours were concerned, and it took another 31 years before they again won the domestic title.

Back Again to Winner's Enclosure

But all went well in 1987-88 when Jed-forest won the title after a play off against Kelso at Melrose. Jed were Division 2 champions that year, and Melrose were playing in the top flight, a situation which gave the Riverside faithful additional pleasure.

Outstanding that year were Grant Farquharson, the scrum half who was also remembered at Netherdale, and Gregor McKechnie, a goal kicker whose contribution to the Jed wins were often memorable.

Ronnie Kirkpatrick, one of the legion of stylish and forceful Jed back row men, was another key member of the side.

As so often in later years, Jed could blow hot and cold, often within a week, but they got it all right on a memorable evening at The Greenyards in the play-off against old rivals Kelso.

Only another seven years were to pass before Jed-forest picked up their seventh, and to date, their last Border League title.

Season 1994-5 saw a side in which the permanently sprightly Harry Hogg teamed up with Kevin Amos to give the Riverside club a robust but still cutting edge on the right.

Chris Richards was beginning to look very much the part at full back in many games, but the formidable back row of Kevin Liddle, Callum Brown and Ronnie Kirkpatrick was probably Jed-forest's strongest unit.

It was well on in April before the League could be settled, but the Jed folk didn't mind waiting.

The nearest the Royal Blues came to further success was in reaching the play-off stage against Hawick in the last competition of the first hundred years. They didn't make it, but they still have the best record of the South country teams after Hawick and Melrose.

The Big Match

Cheers, Tears, and Jethart's Here

The two old rivals from the banks of the Jed and the Tweed had a rare set-to in season 1987-8. There had been little between them all year, and when the last game of the League programme ended in a win for Jedforest by 10-12 they found themselves tied for the top place - with identical records of won seven, drawn two and lost three.

So it was off to The Greenyards for a play-off game that surpassed all expectations. There had been many occasions when a critical game had seen both teams seize up, but not on this occasion.

By the end of the night "Jethart's Here" was ringing out in the Melrose clubrooms, with captain Harry Hogg and president Bill Mabon in ecstasy, Roy Laidlaw achieving one of his greatest rugby ambitions, and Bill Purdie in tears in the dressing room.

The first play-off in the League for 62 years was a fitting match, with Laidlaw setting up the opening try for Brian Hughes with a typical sniping run, Ker replying with a drop goal, and Gregor McKechnie edging Jed further ahead with a penalty goal. Ker kicked a penalty for Kelso but McKechnie added one for Jed and the interval came with a 10-6 scoreline.

The big Melrose crowd - and there were many neutrals there - saw Kelso go into what seemed a commanding lead with a Ker try, conversion and penalty. Kelso were after their third title in a row, and Jed for their first since 1957, and it was the black and whites who looked the likelier side.

But it was Roy Laidlaw, the old hand, who took charge. He had moved to stand-off, found a link, and Brian Hughes was in at the corner for his second try.

Near, but not near enough for Jed at 15-14 against them. But Gregor McKechnie, who had missed five of his last seven kicks at goal, recovered his form when faced with the ultimate challenge.

He thumped the conversion over from the corner, Jed endured a few more moments of pounding from Kelso, but then it was time for the singing, the cheers and the tears to start.

Roy Laidlaw of Jed-forest and John Rutherford of Selkirk - Border League rivals who teamed up for the South and Scotland

LANGHOLM

SINGLE WIN A HAPPY MEMORY

That Langholm have but one success in the Border League to their credit after a hundred years of competition still seems a bit hard on one of the founding fathers of the game in this part of Scotland.

The club's influence, right from the start, has been profound, and their solitary win - in 1958-9 - was thoroughly deserved, and richly celebrated.

Langholm, as much as any club, extended the game of rugby football around their own area of Dumfriesshire, and over the Border.

They were an attractive and strong side when the original five Border clubs set up the league in 1901-2, and it was their influence, as much as any other Border club, which brought Carlisle into the Border competition in 1904.

The first years of the century were strong ones for Langholm, and they were often in the hunt for Border League honours, without ever being able to contain the likes of Jed-forest, who enjoyed so much early success.

Names such Tom Scott and J.V. Goodfellow featured in one of the fastest back divisions in Scotland, and Jim Elliot, bearing an honourable name in the annals of Langholm rugby, was one of the outstanding forwards.

When Langholm's own standards began to decline just before the first world war their hopes of Border League success faded too. And by the time of the twenties the economic prosperity of the town had declined, and with it the quality of the local rugby.

Calling in the Army

Players were often in short supply and desperate measures were needed to keep the team at full strength. At one time these included drafting in some servicemen from the barracks in Carlisle to make up a team to meet Hawick.

Sadly, no one asked them their names, and they go down in the Langholm records as "three unknown soldiers".

Around this time there occurred one of the rare distinctions of a father and son playing in the same Border League game. J Goodfellow, Sen., and J. Goodfellow, junior, turned out against Kelso as members of the back division, father being the full back.

Langholm 1st XV 1919-1920.
Back row: J. Wilson, C. Elliot, R. Irving, A. A. Gray, J. Bell, J. W. Common.
Front row: J. J. Beattie, B. Black, J. V. Goodfellow, J. Hotson (capt.), T. G. Elliot, L. Beattie, R. B. Beattie.
In front: W. Ross and W. A. Lightbody.

Slowly Langholm began to build up their strength from within, but they were more often than not at the bottom of the League table at the season's end.

Langholm have owed a lot to several local families whose names are a permanent part of the club's history, and it was the Armstrongs, Copelands, Bells, and McGlassons who wielded great influence on the club and sustained it in difficult times.

Much of the Langholm enthusiasm was generated by the Scottish internationalist the Rev. J.L. Cotter, the local minister for many years, who encouraged the new generations after the second world war.

The Border League agreed to mark Langholm's 75th anniversary with a game in 1947 between a combined Hawick and Langholm side versus the rest of the League.

Names like Hector Monro and Jim Telford appear in the combined side, and a memorable night ended with a celebration dinner in the Eskdale Hotel.

Langholm began to find the right players for key positions as the fifties dawned but could still not crack the Border League problem, despite the appearance of Christy Elliot, Jimmy Maxwell and Tony Grieve which gave them a cutting edge behind the scrum envied by many other clubs.

Waiting for the Big One

The famous "waterside" crowd, such a feature of games at Milntown Park, continued to go with the flow of the game, following the line out play down the touchline as a succession of visiting sides began to find it harder and harder to pick up wins.

At the start of 1958-9 there was an air of expectation in their ranks.

British Lion Ernie Michie, a giant by the standards of the local game, had come to work in the forestry industry in the area, and joined Langholm to add a missing element to the team - and one which was to prove crucial in a memorable year.

Selkirk were first to be put to the sword by 40 points.

Melrose, Hawick, Gala, and Jed-forest were the next Border sides who found the fired up Langholm side the most forbidding of opponents. The Milntown side carried three internationalists in Michie, Elliot and Maxwell, but that was only part of the story.

Towards the end of the season Langholm were the only unbeaten team in Britain, out of the 420 clubs listed in the national press.

The season was becoming slightly unreal, bearing in mind Langholm's years of unsuccessful endeavour, but the local population was living and breathing rugby in a way they never had before.

Langholm then defeated the visiting London Scottish, and with confidence riding high they went on to clinch the Border League title for the first and only time in their history.

In one of the League's featured games they went to The Greenyards at the end of April, 1959, and left victorious.

League Champions Langholm in 1958-9
Back row: W. Murray, G. H. Sadler, J. B. Copeland A. Irving, G. Crawford,
E. J. S. Michie, J. Beattie, G. Maxwell, J. G. Smith, J. T. Donaldson, J. Telford.
Front row: A. J. Jeffrey, T. G. Elliot, A. D. Warwick, R. Wylie, J. A. Turnbull,
J. M. Maxwell (Capt.), I. Fletcher, C. Elliot, D. I. Anderson, J. K. Armstrong,
T. Grieve, J. G. Elliot.
In front: C. A. March and G. K. Davidson.

Christy Elliot kept his head down, his eye on the ball, and sent over three fine penalties for a 9-6 win and the start of the biggest party in Langholm's history.

Hector Monro, by the happiest of chances the president of the Border League that year, had enormous pride in presenting the trophy to Jimmy Maxwell.

The club had never had the greatest playing strength in Scotland, but always made good use of their resources. That year they used a squad of only 25 men.

It was too much to expect Langholm to stay at the top after such a season and with the inevitable retirals they fell away in the League competition.

But there were still some splendid moments for Langholm's loyal support to savour.

In 1970-2 Stephen Turk, captain that year, led the team to a victory at Mansfield Park, never an easy ground for any visiting side.

He kicked a penalty goal and then Christy Elliot ran in for the only try of the match in the 22nd season since he had first played for the club.

Langholm, as much as any club in the Borders, have a family tradition that has served them well. The names ring like a roll call of Border Reivers down the years- the Elliots, the Armstrongs, the Maxwells and many others - names as rich in Langholm rugby as in Border heritage.

The Big Match

Christy Elliot Makes Sure

Fifteen happy Langholm lads were carried off the field at The Greenyards by their jubilant supporters on an April evening in 1959.

It hadn't been the greatest game ever - and compared to some of Langholm's matches that year it had, frankly, been a bit colourless - but it brought them the Border League title for the first, and so far, the only time in a century of Border competition.

Three penalty goals to two tries usually raises a doubt as to whether the result has gone the right way, but it would have been a bold man - and a pretty ungracious one - who grudged Langholm their win.

There was more than just the Border League going for Langholm that night - there was the unofficial Scottish championship as well, and the distinction of being the only undefeated side in British senior rugby at the end of season 1958-9.

With the result remaining in doubt until the very end the game made up in excitement what it lacked in class. Melrose forwards were the stronger, but Langholm, who had hunted like ferrets all season, produced some fine cover defence particularly through Jimmy Maxwell and Christy Elliot.

Alec "Moose" Hastie was the star for Melrose. His solo try after 25 minutes balanced Elliot's 40 yard penalty ten minutes earlier, and then Elliot edged Langholm ahead with another penalty just before the break.

The second half was as close as the first, and even when Elliot put over a 35 yard penalty Melrose came back at them and threequarter Andrew Hewat scored the home side's second try.

It was the way of things in the fifties and sixties for games to go all the way to the wire, especially when it was a tight affair at the top, and so it was again at The Greenyards.

Hastie, not often given to such excesses, went for a drop goal in the final minutes, but it was never a winner, and the end came with Langholm, although breathing deeply, the top team in Britain.

Little surprise that Hector Monro, president of Langholm and the Border League, took, as they say, great pleasure in handing over the Cup to Jimmy Maxwell.

That of course was only the start of the fun, and when Langholm reached home late that night they were met by two bands, 1500 of their townsfolk on the streets, and the party was only just beginning.

MEMORIES FROM THE MINUTES

In 1920 the Border League committee, perhaps looking far ahead, and being possessed of a charitable spirit, asked the S.R.U. to consider reinstating disabled professionals as they could be of use to clubs or committees. This proposal could not be considered by the Union who rejected it with the observation that "they regretted that the Border League should have made such a proposal."

In 1966 a proposal that the Border League fixtures be dropped from double to single was soundly rejected by the committee.

As recently as 1988 Border League committee members "viewed with some scepticism the fact that prizes in cash might be given at some time in the distant future at Border sevens".

The best traditions of the league were demonstrated in 1950 when a Kelso-Melrose game was abandoned with 25 minutes to go, and Melrose leading 15-3. Kelso suggested this should go down as a win for Melrose.

The customary thanks from the retiring president of the Border League were generally predictable, but on one occasion in the 1990s he was reported as acknowledging the work of two of his senior colleagues in changing his taste from white to red wine!

MELROSE

A BIG FINISH TO THE CENTURY

It may have taken Melrose the greater part of the century to get into the habit of winning the Border League - they managed only two outright wins in the first 50 years - but they have finished far away the most consistent performers in the last decade.

With wins in seven of the last eleven seasons Melrose have shown an appetite for success that only Hawick have matched.

And as the League celebrates a hundred years of local rivalry in the Borders it's worth remembering that it was a Melrose man, J.E. Fairbairn, who was charged with the job of negotiating with the Scottish Football Union to get the Border League recognised.

He made such a good job of it that the authorities in Edinburgh offered to put up the greater part of the money for the Cup.

Melrose seldom showed up well in the early days and it was only after a play-off in 1910-11 that they picked up their first championship.

Melrose had just beaten Jed-forest for the first time in 20 years, scoring what was regarded in those days as a decisive win by 6-0, with tries from J. Bunyan and W. Douglas.

Big Crowd for Decider

This set up a deciding game against Hawick at Riverside, and it proved a great finish to the season. Riverside Park housed almost a record crowd, Melrose winning 10-0 with tries by Lowrie both converted by Davidson,

The Melrose team had a great reception on returning home, not surprisingly, and were met at the station by a large crowd.

Wattie Douglas, the local grocer and team captain, was carried shoulder high and two pipers led the company to the Market Square "where there was much cheering".

The club President, the same J.E. Fairbairn, had the pleasure of seeing his missionary work five years earlier paying off for his own club.

The first Melrose side to win the League title in 1910-11
Back row: J. Crawford (Trainer), R. Williamson (Secretary), W. J. Turner (Secretary), James Brown (Treasurer).
Standing: J. E. Fairbairn (President), J. C. Haig, D. Bunyan, G. Ballantyne, J. Brown, R. Davidson, B. Yea, Dr Ross, J. H. Lawrie (Vice-President).
Seated: J. Gill, J. Lawrie, J. Jardine, W. Douglas (Captain), J. J. Fairbairn, M. Jardine, W. Shiel, W. Black.
In front: J. Bunyan, J. Hunter.

What brought Melrose success that particular year must have been a special kind of hunger, off the field as well as on - for that was the season when the committee had decided unanimously that the provision of tea at away matches be withdrawn from the first fifteen, while being given to the seconds.

Personalties in that Melrose side were local tradesmen Jock Jardine, who kicked the goals and was vice captain, and Bob Davidson, who ran a draper's shop in the town.

After that success Melrose toiled for many years with much honest endeavour but without picking up the trophy again.

Local issues concerned the committee, and an indication of how the Border clubs of the time depended on the local train services comes from a 1921 minute of the Melrose club.

It was proposed that action should be taken with regard to the non-stopping of the 1.12 p.m. and 4.5 p.m. expresses from Carlisle to Edinburgh at Melrose. What the action was, and how successful the outcome is not now clear, but clearly the train service was of vital importance to teams and spectators.

Games early in the century generally started later than nowadays, and it was quite usual for teams to leave by train for an away game as late as 3 p.m.

Gala Supporters Get Red Card

Another issue concerned relationships with near neighbours and onetime club mates Gala. A first fifteen game against Gala at Netherdale in the early 1920s was described as the scene of disgraceful behaviour on the part of the Gala spectators.

The game ended in a 6-6 draw but the Melrose minutes record what must have been a heated discussion "The least thing a Melrose player did, which did not please the spectators, they booed and hissed them and asked that they be put off the field."

Gala's minutes are quiet on the issue.

Melrose achieved very little between the wars, finishing second in 1933-4, but gradually the team's standard began to improve, particularly behind the scrum.

Up front it was characters like Jock Allan who strove valiantly but it was a period in Scottish rugby when the class backs were in the city sides.

But with the approach of the second World War Melrose put it all right in season 1938-9.

The first game against Gala ended in defeat by 11-9, but Melrose nearly pulled it off in the last minute. A move started on their own line was just foiled as Lawson Drummond was hauled down by the Gala defence.

It was regarded by many shrewd judges as one of the finest Border League games seen at the Greenyards for a very long time.

This set the standard of play that was going to bring the Border League Cup to Melrose come April.

The deciding game of the season for the League was played at Philiphaugh on a Thursday evening, Melrose winning 19-5. Frank Smart had two of the four tries with Jock Allan and Lawson adding the others. Allan converted two and kicked a penalty.

It was the first Melrose win in the League for 29 years.

Melrose Miss Out on Three Void Years

The post-war years started bleakly, with the Border League committee having no choice but to declare three championships void because of a back log of fixtures which couldn't be cleared. By coincidence Melrose were involved in the tight finishes of all three.

Season 1946-7 is still regarded as one of the worst of the century in weather terms, and for eight successive weeks no club rugby could be played. Melrose were leading the abbreviated league table when it was finally declared void having beaten both Hawick and Gala, the nearest challengers, in away games.

The following season the weather relented, but the tightest of finishes saw Melrose, Jed-forest and Kelso all locked together in a situation that allowed no prospect of a decision. All three clubs had identical records of played 12, won 7, lost 3 and drawn 2.

That season, incidentally, was the final one for the four point drop goal and Melrose, in their match against Selkirk, made the most of it, with four drop goals to one from their opponents.

Season 1949-50 saw the two old rivals Melrose and Gala locked in a struggle which ended all square, the title being shared. Gala led for most of the season, but Melrose recovered from a poor start when the injured Alastair Frater was badly missed.

At the end of March Gala, Hawick and Melrose had all a chance, but Melrose saw off Hawick with two Ivor Hogg penalty goals to earn a 6-5 win.

Robin Chisholm and Charlie Drummond performed heroics in defence and it was on to Netherdale for the decider, a game postponed from January.

The game fell flat in a drawn game, the season was wearing on, and there was no hope of a further game to settle the title.

The Greenyards men won the unofficial championship in 1951-2 but the Border League again could not be completed.

Bad weather in the first months of 1952 saw six Saturday games unplayed but even so Melrose were in a strong position with seven wins and a draw in eight games when the League committee blew the whistle on the competition.

It was hard luck on Melrose, who were celebrating their 75 year and who were the outstanding Scottish side, winning the unofficial championship.

However most of the Melrose side were still around in 1953-4 and they had a grand run against the other Border sides.

Leslie Allan dropped a goal to beat Hawick 3-0 and button up the League, and in the return game against the Teries the same score came through a George Lackie penalty goal.

The only blemishes on the Melrose card were a defeat by Jed-forest and a draw at Langholm after the title was won.

Low Scoring Marked Melrose Win

The whole season was a tight affair, and not a single side managed to score a hundred points in the League. So it was no surprise when Melrose, winning their first outright title since the second world war, did the double over Selkirk with scores of only 9-3 and 12-3. Cutting loose, they wrapped it up at Kelso with a 14-3 win.

Robin Chisholm captained the side, with Alastair Frater, Jack Dun, Leslie Allan, Jimmy Johnston, Ogilvie Scott and Derek Brown some of the other personalities.

Season 1957-8 was badly hit by the weather and at the end of March only 28 out of 42 League games had been played. But Hector Monro of Langholm, president of the League, insisted that every effort be made to finish it and Melrose seized the chance.

The Border League had abandoned their previous insistence that all games should be over by April 15th, and a new fixture list was drawn up. It meant Melrose having four away games in a fortnight, and in winning them all they produced a stamina sapping performance that deservedly earned them the title.

It was Derek Brown's year as captain, and in a stirring game at Hawick he followed David Chisholm's penalty goal and drop goal by dribbling from half field to score the game's only try.

With wins at Kelso and Netherdale, Melrose had to go to Philiphaugh on the last day of April, and struggled for much of the game before three late tries brought them a victory and their latest League title.

The next time Melrose won the League title they were led by David Chisholm, and they added the Scottish championship to the local honours in season 1962-3. All the Border clubs had endured a winter of bad weather, and many of the games were a bit of an ordeal.

League Champions Melrose in 1962-3
Standing: J. Crawford (President), W. M. Brown, T. E. Allan, M. Fairbairn, D, A. Hogg, J. W, Telfer, J. Crawford, F. A. L. Laidlaw, N. Elliot, G. Tweedie, R. R. Brown (Secretary).
Seated: D. M, Brown, R, W. T. Chisholm, W. E. Allan, D. H. Chisholm (Captain), R. Blacklock, A. Hastie, W. Hart.

Hawick had looked like running away with the title, and were scoring freely although they squeezed home against Melrose at Mansfield by only 6-3. Melrose caught them up when Gala earned a draw against the Greens, and another of the Border League's most celebrated games settled the issue at The Greenyards.

Great Game Brought Narrow Melrose Win

It was one of the most splendid matches ever to grace the Border League. Hawick came to The Greenyards for a game that ended 5-0 for the home side, a classic match that is still talked over by Border rugby folk. It was watched by a crowd of around 4,000, as were a number of the big games in these days.

The game itself gave Melrose the space they needed. With Hawick losing again to Langholm, within seven days. and Melrose beating

Jed-forest, the men from The Greenyards then produced wins over Langholm and Selkirk to lift the title.

It was the last match of his career for Robin Chisholm, and he scored a fine try.

The year 1970-1 broke a long sequence of Hawick wins, and Melrose, under Jim Telfer's captaincy for the sixth and last time, picked up their next success.

League Champions Melrose in 1970-1
Back row: J. B. Mitchell, A. Wilson, J. L. Redpath, B. Chalmers, G. R. Barkham,
    J. N. C. Elliot, D. Semple, D. Pringle,
Standing: H. M. Pollock, J. Frater, G. Blyth, L Rutherford, M. Kaczynski, K. W. Dodds,
    J. M. Sharp, R. Oliver, W. Mitchellhill, J. A. Hardie, M. F. Fairbairn.
Seated: W. E. Allan, J. T. Blacklock, T. E. Allan, J. W. Telfer (Captain),
    D. M. Hogg (President), F. A. L. Laidlaw, G. D. Tweedie.
In front: E. Brown, J. C. Wheelans, K. Turner, R. A. Lind
(T. D. Wight and P. J. Bird absent)

Both the Hawick games were dominated by penalties, and Melrose's outstanding performance was the 17-16 win over Kelso. But the most memorable match was the home game against Gala when the Maroons won 14-16.

Melrose celebrated their latest title, but that was it, until the golden years which arrived at the start of the nineties. The first of these seasons, 1989-90, was something special, with Melrose, under Keith Robertson's captaincy, winning the Border League before the turn of the year, the first team ever to do so.

The names of Craig Chalmers, Bryan Redpath, and Graham Shiel were some of the local internationalists produced by Melrose as they won five league titles in a row.

The Border League cup seemed permanently on display in The Greenyards, and with the face of rugby changing rapidly a succession of captains presided over a team of all the talents.

There were new names in the yellow and black, many of them unfamiliar ones to The Greenyards faithful.

But with Robbie Brown, the fourth generation of his family to play for Melrose, and members of the great Melrose families of Crawfords, Allans, Fraters, Taits and Laidlaws still contributing to the Greenyards story, there was a clear impression that some things were not for changing.

The Big Match

Top Form Melrose Take Trophy

Melrose turned out for their match against Selkirk in April, 1963, as the hottest favourites for many a day.

They had the prospect of their first double triumph in the League and the unofficial championship as the prize for winning, and made sure from the opening minutes just how much they fancied their chances.

Selkirk, on the other hand, had endured a pretty miserable season, and hadn't scored a single point against Border opposition all winter.

It was, then, an unequal struggle on paper, and so it proved. Alec Hastie sent in his captain David Chisholm for the opening try, but then Selkirk delighted their supporters with a try by Eric Hislop, converted by Gerald Beggs.

David Chisholm and Alec Hastie, teammates for Melrose and Scotland

The excitement began to build up - it was the first time that Selkirk had taken the lead against a Scottish side all season.

Melrose were in no mood to be generous, despite some ferocious Selkirk tackling, but it took until after the interval before the favourites managed to shake themselves free.

When the Selkirk full back was caught in possession Wat Hart pounced on a desperate pass and scored. Robin Chisholm finished off a move initiated by brother David, and the Melrose forwards began to secure control.

Jim Telfer, Wat Hart and the Brown brothers were in rampant form, and Melrose rattled in more points with a try by Mac Brown, and a conversion and drop by David Chisholm.

Mike Cipolato and Wat Hart added tries, and that was it......one of the easier Border League victory games, but Melrose were clearly the team of the year.

Such was their superiority at the time that it was a great surprise when the team could manage only one more success in the League until their great run began more than 30 years after that big night against Selkirk.

CARLISLE

THE CUMBERLAND CONNECTION

Naming the teams of the Border League is nowadays the easiest of questions for anyone in a rugby quiz.

But ask which team was in the competition with Gala, Hawick, Melrose, Langholm and Jed-forest, long before Kelso and Selkirk, and nearly 90 years before Peebles, and the answer is not so easy.

It was in fact Carlisle, who had one and a half seasons in the original competition away back in 1904-5.

Carlisle involvement in the League developed from their lengthy connection with Langholm, the two sides meeting for the first time as far back as 1873, in Carlisle's first ever game. They started that day the longest cross border series of club fixtures anywhere in the rugby world, and one which is still played today.

When the Border clubs started putting together their championship in the first years of the century, Carlisle were already making occasional forays across the Border. They had been playing Gala, for one, since 1887, and it was a logical move to include them in the league table.

Rugby south of the Border in these days was a fairly basic pastime, and Carlisle one of the most down to earth places to play it.

The town was a rugby stronghold and the game, according to local sages, was exciting to play. For a long time there was no referee and no one to whistle up if things got out of hand.

The simple rule was that if one player annoyed another - and the players made a habit of annoying each other - they retired behind the pavilion to settle the difference with fists. Sometimes as many as four or five fights were in progress at the same time. But the game went on.

Carlisle appear to have had only one complete season in the Border league table, and just why they dropped out so quickly is hard to establish.

It certainly wasn't because of a poor record.

As late as the middle of March, with the 1904-5 season drawing to an end, they were ahead of both Langholm and Melrose. But the fixture list was far from balanced, with some teams playing only four games to the ten of their opponents.

It's thought that the Border clubs were anxious to tighten up the competition, and there were plans to have teams play each other thrice, with two of the games counting as competitive matches and the third a friendly.

The most likely reason for Carlisle's departure, midway through the season, was that the Scottish clubs were already laying plans to have their championship fully recognised by the Scottish Football Union.

It seems quite likely that as they prepared for their formal approach to Edinburgh they realised that the chances of success would be greater if they confined the new structure to the five active senior Border clubs.

Certainly the timing suggests this may have been the reason, but whatever it was Carlisle's disappearance was abrupt and uncharted.

They were handily placed at the end of December, 1905, with two wins out of their three games, but over the New Year period something fairly dramatic occurred and the first table of 1906 makes no mention at all of the Carlisle record.

No reference to the affair appears in the Carlisle minutes, and, coupled with the suggestion that extensive travelling was presenting problems, the conclusion has to be reached that there were no great regrets about the parting of the ways.

A Veteran Remembers

According to Tom Scott, one of their most loyal members who was associated with them as a player, office bearer and supporter for 68 years, Carlisle's connection with the Scottish Border clubs did much to enhance their standing in England.

The quality of the games against Langholm, Gala, Hawick and Melrose, even after they no longer were connected through the Border competition, did much to ensure that Carlisle emerged as the leading side in Cumberland.

Shortly before he died in the summer of 2000 Tom Scott recalled the work that he and other early enthusiasts did to build Carlisle into their position as the standard bearer for English rugby in the north west corner of the land.

Born just eight years after Carlisle had played in the Border competition, Tom Scott started playing as a schoolboy and remembered older members of the club telling him of the journeys they made in the early days to play the Border sides.

Even Langholm was a lengthy trip at the turn of the century, and visits to Melrose and Galashiels were verging on journeys into the unknown.

Tom Scott could throw no light on why the Carlisle connection with the Border competition was so short, but suspected that the travelling times had something to do with it.

He acknowledged too that the Border clubs may have wanted to keep the new League as an all-Scottish affair, but fixtures continued on an irregular basis, and there was clearly no ill-feeling.

Whatever the reason, Carlisle faded from the Border League scene, leaving behind memories of a short spell in the Border spotlight.

But had the bid to formalise the league competition been made to the English as well as the Scottish ruling body, and had the clubs been able to overcome the travelling problems, would Carlisle have remained the only English side involved ?

Perhaps the turn of the century would have seen a celebration of a League centenary covering both sides of the Border.

The Hunt's Up

Riverside Park was the scene of one of the more unusual interruptions ever seen in a Border League game.

During play a fox sped across the field, hotly pursued by a pack of hounds, and then by the entire hunt.

Both the Jed-forest and Selkirk teams, caught up in the excitement, abandoned play and rushed to the river embankment to see the end of the chase, leaving referee Billy Burnet of Hawick pondering whether to add extra time to the match.

Frank Reporting

According to press reports in the early years of the century the Melrose backs included a "swift sort of chap in D. Bunyan, but one into whose arms the ball had to be placed and who had to be told to run for all he's fit!"

The same player, who was obviously someone to keep your eye on, was described in the same report as "when the others are knee deep in mud, Dave while's does something startling".

 # SELKIRK

YEARS OF WAITING END IN SUCCESS

Selkirk came late to the Border League - their formal admittance not being until 1908 - but they had as long a pedigree as anyone in the Borders, even if the line had been broken more than once.

What was the forerunner of many a Border derby took place in 1877 when Selkirk met Galashiels, as their neighbours were billed, on the cricket field, the first match played in Selkirk under rugby rules.

A Selkirk side went on to play senior rugby during the 1890's in what was a very full fixture list against Gala, Hawick, Melrose and other Border clubs, and had no fewer than 24 games in the last season of the century.

But rugby in the town took a tumble as the new century dawned. As several other clubs in the district began to draw together in the first organised rugby league in the world, Selkirk were missing out.

At the start of the twentieth century trade in the town was depressed, players were leaving for the professional game, and association football was getting more popular.

Selkirk were not the only team to suffer, but they had to revert to junior status and had a few unhappy years while the other Border sides were getting established in the new league.

Had Selkirk hung on for one year the chances are they would have been in at the start of the Border Championship, and it might not have taken until 1934-5 for their first League success.

But shortly after joining Selkirk were already taking a leading role in the affairs of the League and Mr. G.S. Scott of the town was appointed President in 1911-12. He was also the unanimous choice of the committee to represent the South on the committee of the Scottish Football Union.

The years immediately after the first World War were vintage ones for Selkirk rugby and it was at this time that a Hawick worthy said "if we had yon Selkirk backs and they Hawick forrits, we'd lick a' creation."

Classy backs were all very well, but it took the arrival of one of Selkirk's most powerful packs from the years between the wars to bring the Souters their first Border League championship, in 1934-5.

Solid Scrummaging Brought Anniversary Success

It was a pack which turned on solid Scottish scrummaging of the old school, playing together in a tight and powerful blend.

Like so many other teams who enjoyed success in the League, Selkirk couldn't get through with a clean slate, and two games were lost. But in the 400th year of celebrating the town's oldest existing Royal charter the League title was a fine bonus.

It was a game at the Greenyards which saw Selkirk home for their first League triumph. They won by 17 points to 14, and the winning team was led by Bob Edgar, a fine strapping forward who led a formidable pack.

Other memorable figures were Stewart Roberts, who missed out on international selection because of poor eyesight, Jock Beattie, Wull Wilson and Tom Henderson, all men over six feet in height at a time when the average was distinctly less.

Jack Waters played 16 times for Scotland, and Stewart Roberts went on to become Provost of the Royal and Ancient Burgh. But he was as proud of Selkirk that night in Melrose as at any other time in his distinguished career.

Others in the Selkirk team still remembered today were Bert Lawrie, sprint champion Arthur Murray who featured in Scottish trials, drop goal specialist George "Jim" Roberts, and the regular goal kicker Bob Coultherd.

The winning of the League was celebrated of course with a dinner in the town, one of the guests being Mr. A.A. Lawrie, president elect of the S.R.U.

The Union had occasionally been criticised for failing to recognise the importance of the Border League with its emphasis on winning a title, but on this occasion Mr. Lawrie actually referred to the "championship" in a speech which did much to extend the League's wider credibility.

Not that there was any doubt in Selkirk about the team's achievement.

Selkirk slipped back from their League form in the next couple of seasons but brought together a remarkable team in 1937-8 when they not only took the top Border honours, but nearly the unofficial championship as well.

The S.R.U. might have been able to stomach the former by this time, but still were not too happy with the idea of all the Scottish teams vying for top honours.

Nearly A Double at Philiphaugh

That team of 1937-8 was captained by Alex. Stewart, who had played in the League championship four years earlier. He was a miser when it came to handing out points to the opposition, and their season's record showed scarcely five points a game being lost.

It was far from being the most open rugby ever played by a Selkirk side, but there was plenty excitement with five games being drawn in the League, including both matches against Gala.

Selkirk carried a lot of pace that year, with Border amateur sprint champions Jack Edwards and Stan Carss. At half back were Willie Lees and Stewart Horsburgh, and among the other players were Dod Anderson who had joined the successful Selkirk side from Netherdale, and Jim Bunyan.

But if Selkirk had justified the faith of the loyal Philiphaugh supporters by winning the Border League in 1934-5, and then the League with an accompanying near miss in the unofficial championship four years later they capped it all in 1952-3.

Memories Still Strong After 50 Years

Nearly half a century has now gone by since these heady days when the Souters did the double for the first and only time in their history. But the names of the formidable team are still familiar, and not only at Philiphaugh.

Selkirk and Peebles in Border League action.   (Southern Reporter)

There have been many powerful front rows in the story of the Border League, but Jim "Basher" Inglis, Jock King and George Downie are still recalled as the rock on which the Selkirk double was founded.

It became a point of principle for the Selkirk pack to control the game, and while the backs were seldom able to cut totally loose they made good use of the ball.

Full back Archie Little had come from Walkerburn to play full back for Selkirk, and turned in many a stylish and immaculate performance.

His goal kicking carried the team through some of their closest encounters, and he showed many of the cavalier touches which were seen in mature terms in the play of later full backs such as Kenny Scotland and Andy Irvine. In many ways Archie Little was before his time.

The crunch games for Selkirk in that memorable season came in the last two matches, against Gala and Jed-forest. Tom Brown had kicked an early drop goal against Gala, who were also in with a chance of League honours, and the team survived intense pressure from the Maroons to win 3-0.

It was Archie Little's turn to be the match winner in the final game against Jed-forest when his solitary penalty goal was the only score of the night. The side survived against the Foresters when a last minute drop goal attempt went wide.

But Selkirk's historic side broke up quickly and Border League success became a thing of memory.

With players like John Rutherford and Gordon Hunter at half back, and some talented threequarters, Selkirk were often an attractive team to watch, but they found it hard to reproduce the forward strength and control that marked the great season of 1952-3.

The Big Match

Archie Little Wraps Up League Trophy

The tension had been building for a week or more before the Selkirk side emerged on to the Philiphaugh pitch on a Wednesday night late in April, 1953.

All that was needed to produce their first Border League win since 1937-8 was a win against Jed-forest, hardy enough competitors but not that year quite of the calibre of a Selkirk side which was also eyeing the Scottish unofficial championship.

Like many another vital game at a critical time, this match saw the potential champions seize up.

The crowd was big, the conditions far from unpleasant, but Selkirk took an unconsciously long time to settle.

One of the stars of their season, Stanley Cowan, had an off night, but every excuse, with both his thumbs dislocated early on. Long before the days of replacements he had little choice but to stay on the field, and it was this commitment that did much to lift the spirits of the team.

And when George Mitchell of Jed-forest, ironically a Souter himself, had to be carried off in the second half with a leg injury the local crowd must have thought that at last the luck was going their way.

Selkirk did much of the attacking throughout the entire game, but flashes of excitement were few indeed, and their handling let them down badly.

Archie Little, from up Tweeddale way, who had settled into the full back berth at Philiphaugh, was the saviour of the day. In the second half he kicked a fine penalty goal - all the finer because of the nervous tension that was building up around the ropes. And for the entire game he showed a coolness under the Jed pressure that steadied the uncertain Selkirk side.

Jed were far and away the livelier side, their backs, with winger Elliot and scrum half Cairns outstanding, going about their business with a lot more certainty than Selkirk.

As the long night wore on Selkirk began to take a bit more control up front, and with Little's goal in the bag the more optimistic supporters began to see the first Border League success for 16 years drawing near.

But there was still a sting in the tale of a game which meant so much to Selkirk.

Jed had lifted their game again, full back Alex Bell glanced at the Selkirk posts and launched a long distance drop goal attempt. While the Selkirk faithful looked on in dismay the ball headed for the posts and then grazed the upright —on the wrong side for Jed-forest.

A tight finish, a close run thing, but Selkirk were home in what turned out to be their last Border League victory of the century. There was a happy gathering in the County Hotel after the game, with four of Selkirk's internationalists, Willie Bryce, Jock Waters, Jock King, and "Basher" Inglis all present to enjoy the celebrations.

League champions Selkirk in 1952 -3
Back row - J. Anderson, Treasurer, T.P. Brown, S. Macdonald, J. Dalgleish, S. Cowan, J. Cowan.
Second T. Henderson, chairman, W. Waters, J.M. Inglis, G. Russell, D.W. Walker, G. Sykes, A.D. Little, W. Hamilton, W. Blake, J.A.F. Beattie, Secretary.
Third J. Cowan, P. Wright, D. Burrell, G. Downie, captain, J.F. King, H. Wilson J. Heatlie.
Front T. Heatlie, A. Wyse, S.O.Russell, W.D. Nichol

 # KELSO

A LONG WAIT WELL WORTH WHILE

Kelso were late arrivals on the Border League scene, and the initial impact they made was far from being dramatic.

It took until 1912 for them to join in, a world war came and went, and eleven more years passed, before they had their first sniff of the silverware.

When Kelso became members they had already been in existence since 1876. Games often took place against some of the well established teams, but the fixture list tended to feature games against second fifteens and junior sides around the Borders.

But it was a win over Hawick by a try to nil, and then a match against Melrose in 1911-12 that really set them up for the big time.

Kelso won 7-0, a convincing enough win in those days, but especially significant in that Melrose had won the Border League the previous season.

On February 9th, 1912, the townsfolk turned out in big numbers to debate the question of Kelso joining what was known as the Senior League. Despite worries about the financing of the new deal, the meeting was in no doubt.

The club had enjoyed their success against Melrose, and an overwhelming majority voted for joining the Border League. It took the League committee only until May to accept the Kelso application.

Setting the Shepherds Cheering

Now firmly established as a senior club, Kelso lost their first game in 1912-13 to Jed-forest but pulled off a great win a few weeks later when they beat Hawick at home.

It was said that the result was telegraphed to the Yetholm Shepherds' Show where it was received "amid enthusiastic cheering".

For the return game a fortnight later the North British Railways Company laid on a special train for 500 Kelso supporters, and hundreds more travelled by road.

This was one of the many times that the local railway companies recognised the strength of support for the emerging game of Border rugby.

Years after that first Kelso triumph one of the club's great favourites, Henry Aitchison, could recall being taken as a youngster to see Kelso play in their first season in the Border League.

As his father was president he and his mother were given VIP treatment and provided with a special form to sit on.

Despite being far from impressed by the game, and told off for fidgeting, he went on to become one of Kelso's most influential figures and a regular attender at Poynder Park well into his nineties.

With the war intervening, rugby at Poynder Park was interrupted, but by the time season 1925-6 arrived a new stand had been built, and rugby in the town was on an upward path.

Kelso challenged Hawick all the way for the League title, winning at Mansfield Park for the first time in their history. Jimmy Graham and Jock Hume, the latter one of Kelso's long line of talented stand-offs, were two of the distinguished members of that side.

They went on winning right through the autumn and early winter months, but the run ended on a January afternoon at Poynder Park in the return game with Hawick.

The pitch had to be cleared of snow before the game could go on before an excited crowd of around 3,500, and Hawick withstood some furious Kelso pressure before winning 3-0.

This produced a play-off situation - for the third time in Hawick's history but of course for the first time in the case of Kelso. The game went on at The Greenyards and Hawick got home again to deny Kelso their first title.

After the heroics at Mansfield Park early on in the season, where Kelso were not to win again for 51 years, it was a bit of a let down for the men in black and white, but they were not to be denied too long.

First Time Success

Season 1930-1 brought the breakthrough. Kelso were captained that year by "Flood" Rodgers and with redoubtable forwards such as Jimmy Graham and Gordon Cottington they were a match for most up front.

The first Kelso side to win the Border League in 1930-1
Back Row J.T. Laing (Hon. Secy.), G. Cottingdon, W. Grieve, T. Laidlaw,
J. Graham, J. H. P. Blackadder, W. Hope, A. B. Tully (President).
Centre Row A. G. Cameron, W. A. Smith R. T. Smith, G. Rodgers (Capt.),
R. F. Kennedy, W. R. Caldwell, J. Bennet,
Sitting T. Chalmers, A. Stephenson

Crowds of over 3,000 were not uncommon, and Kelso ploughed on with wins over Hawick, Melrose and Langholm before their first slip up at Netherdale.

Heavy frost put an end to rugby in mid-winter, and Kelso considered protecting the pitch with old railway covers before abandoning the idea on the grounds of cost - nearly £700 and a big sum in the 1930s.

A great run from February took Kelso to the top of the League, and they hung on to meet their closest challengers, Gala, at home in mid-March. A local report of the game described the Kelso pack as being made up of "seven devils, led by Graham, the arch demon."

Gala, a shade peeved at the 8-3 defeat, accused Kelso of rough play, and a bit of rather angry correspondence took place. But in the best traditions of Border rugby it was all forgotten about by the time the summer came along.

Kelso didn't brood on the matter and the club chairman, Mr A.B. Tulley proposed that a celebration dinner be held in the Cross Keys Hotel. Apart from that idea Kelso's first win in the League was greeted quite calmly in the town, probably as being no more than their due.

The team's record in the League was played 11, won 9, lost 2, with 138 points for and 50 against.

Still Winning in the Thirties

After the years of waiting Kelso got two more successes in 1933-4 and 1936-7.

Gordon Cottington was captain in the first of that brace of triumphs, and led the side to six wins in a row. His play earned him a cap against England and a selection for the Barbarians.

Kelso stumbled a bit with losses against Hawick and Gala on two successive weeks, but were able to overcome the traditional warm welcome at Milntown Park and won 16-5 to take the title.

It was not such an overwhelming triumph on this occasion, with a record of played 12, won 8, lost 3, drawn 1, points for totalling only 99 and those against 64.

Mr Tulley, still president, said at the annual meeting that he felt the club would hold on to the League title for a time, and an air of optimism pervaded Poynder Park.

The only blot on the season was the need for the committee to write to one spectator informing him that his conduct at the Kelso-Selkirk match had been such as to require him to be barred from the club's home games until the end of the following season.

Again in the best traditions of Border rugby no grudges were held, and the bar was lifted.

If 1930-1 and 1933-4 had been memorable, Kelso's next season of success 1936-7, was even better, ending up with them fifth in the unofficial Scottish championship, holders of four seven a side cups, and winners of the Border League under the captaincy of W.H. Bookless.

A great run of early success included a convincing win over Hawick, and it looked as though the League would be sewn up before Christmas. But defeats by Jed-forest, and draws against Langholm and Hawick, kept the pot simmering until the final game at Netherdale.

That produced a Doug Lindsay try for Kelso, the only score in the match that secured the title.

Kelso were back in the frame after the war, and nearly added the Border League title to their unofficial championship, won in 1947-8.

A Near Thing at Riverside

But a three way tie resulted from a weather-ruined game at Riverside Park, and the League committee decided that Melrose, Jed-forest and Kelso, all involved in the tight finish, could not be separated that year, and declared the title void.

Kelso remain proud of their record that season, however, and the club's official records claim that the team were joint winners.

A few flurries in the League followed in the next few seasons, and the run of six wins in a row in 1957-8 showed the potential of a side which numbered John Dawson, Roger Baird, Ian Hastie and Ken Smith among its talented members.

But Kelso could not sustain the pace, and years were to pass before further success, even although the "A" team won the Border Junior title in 1959-60 led by the experienced Jock Elliot.

Long years of dominance by Hawick, with occasional interventions from Melrose and Gala, were to go by before Kelso again won the League title.

That came in 1985-6 with a memorable series of matches which included a high scoring double over Gala during a long run of successes against the Maroons.

But a season that brought so much ended with a cloud hanging over the final game.

The Missing Trophy

The title hung on the result of the Melrose-Hawick game at The Greenyards.

Hawick had to win to hold on to the title, but lost to a fired-up Melrose side by 18-9. That handed the trophy to Kelso, but where was it?

Hawick, it turned out, had left the championship trophy at Mansfield Park, and Kelso president Bill Forbes was far from happy. Not only was he the club president, he was president of the Border League as a happy coincidence, and had issued instructions for the trophy to come to Melrose for presentation.

The actual handing-over of the trophy was a bit of an anti climax, and one of the local papers recorded the arrival in Kelso "nearly 50 years after it had last graced the Kelso air."

"The only difference this time around was that the handover was so much different. Two days after the presentation should have been made a van drew up outside the offices of M. and J. Ballantyne in the Sheddon Park Road, and a man was seen carrying a large piece of silver in a plastic bag. It could have been a Co-op bag.

"We can now state that this was the Border League rugby trophy arriving in Kelso..........It arrived in a way that not one Kelso supporter could ever have wished to see happen again, and the Border League committee should take steps to see that such an embarrassing situation should never be allowed to happen again."

With the cup safely delivered, Kelso laid on a party to mark the League title's return after 50 years.

Champagne flowed as former Kelso internationalist, president and club captain Bob Grieve handed over the trophy to Gary Callander. Bob was one of the few survivors of the Kelso side who last won the League in season 1936-7.

However two other members of that line up joined in the celebrations that Saturday night - Allan "Darkie" Smith and Henry Aitchison. Bill Forbes, the president, said that Kelso had won the title as they had taken every other Border league side twice, with the exception of Hawick. "It was a long time since any Kelso team did that."

Of the 27 players used, 22 were in attendance. Bob Grieve described the side as probably the greatest that had ever played for Kelso.

They were certainly amongst the toughest, as in April, 1986, Kelso played three games on four consecutive nights, beating Selkirk, Jed-forest, and Langholm. Seven players played in all three games, and not even at Poynder Park is that likely to be seen again.

The following season, when Kelso won again, the clinching game was at Mansfield Park. Kelso had not won there since the 1925-6 season, but after all the years of disappointment they made no mistake in search of the retention of their title.

League champions Kelso in 1986-7
Back Row - D. L. Martin, A. W. Stewart, A. V. Tait, W. T. Frame, C. D. N. Stewart, G. J. Callander.
Middle Row - B. H. Cuthbert (Match Secretary), R. E. Paxton, I. I. Cassie, A. R. Dick, W. S. Forbes (President), T. G. Waite, A. M. Thomson, A. Hall, K. J. Green, C. E. B. Stewart (Coach).
Front Row - M. R. Minto, N. H. Hastie, D. J. Robeson, G. R. T. Baird (capt), J. Jeffery, R. J. Hogarth, A. B. M. Ker.
Absent S. B. Edwards, R. C. Cowe, M. Wright, G. J. Brown

With a win by 18-12 they collected the trophy under the captaincy of Andrew Ker. It was celebration time again with a function in the clubrooms, when officials, team members and guests enjoyed a party. But that was to be the last Kelso success in the first hundred years of the League.

Late starters they may have been, but when success came few clubs have enjoyed it more.

The Big Match

Cool Ker Sees Kelso Through

The biggest crowd of the season turned out on a Monday night at Poynder Park in April, 1986, to see if Kelso could take a big step towards winning the Border League for the first time since 1937 by beating Hawick.

A victory would guarantee them nothing - it was still going to be left to the games Hawick had to play against Melrose and Langholm if the long-overdue title were to return to Kelso.

But the Monday game was enough to be going on with, and for once the tightness of the occasion did nothing to take the edge off Kelso's game.

It was the coolest player on the field, that day and most days, Andrew Ker, who carried the Tweedsiders through. He steered them to their fourth home win over the Greens in eight seasons, and that was something that not many other Border sides could achieve.

Kelso set about the game convinced that they couldn't lose, and within minutes Dougie Robeson was flying in at the corner. The try was disallowed, there were a few observations from the crowd, but there was worse to come as Kelso missed more chances.

Graeme Brown was off target with four penalties, but Colin Gass was not, and put Hawick three points up against the run of the game.

This was all that Andrew Ker needed, and he set up the game's only try when he looped with Alan Tait after a good Kelso scrum, sending Ewan Common in for a try which Ker converted.

After the break the Kelso faithful sniffed victory in the night air. Ker dropped a goal, Gass missed a penalty attempt and then retired hurt, and the home side piled on the pressure in a frantic last period of the game.

It was, of course, Ker, who slotted the last points with a penalty from an awkward angle, and if they had gone in for such things in the Border League he would have been named man of the match.

As it was, he and the rest of the Kelso side waited patiently for Hawick to lose one of their remaining matches. The League was going all the way to the wire, and there were two matches where Hawick might blow their chances.

Melrose duly obliged Kelso with a heartening win and that produced the League championship for Kelso. But the presentation of the Cup was another matter, told elsewhere in this book.

Action from Melrose v Kelso game during the 1990's   (Southern Reporter)

 # PEEBLES

COME LATE AND WIN EARLY

When Peebles put Selkirk through a torrid finish in their first ever Border League match they showed any doubters just what they were going to bring to the competition.

They had served a long apprenticeship, but showed all the signs of being more than ready for the step up when they played in the League Trophy of season 1995-6.

Peebles were one of the few teams to look kindly upon that curious competition which made a brief and not very impressive appearance in the rugby calendar.

The Border clubs had already been engaged in league competition for 95 years when Peebles were invited to join in 1996, this being the first change to the format since the entry of Selkirk in 1908 and Kelso in 1912.

One of the pleasant things about the Border League has always - or nearly always - been the gentlemanly way in which its business was conducted.

When the time came for Peebles to be admitted the invitation came from the other seven clubs in a courteous letter, and Peebles responded with enthusiasm.

The story of Peebles' growth to their present position as serious competitors in the League really began a long time before their potential was fully realised.

They had been playing other Border clubs for more than a hundred years - their first fixture against Gala for instance was as long ago as 1883 - but the games were far from regular, and the fixture list variable.

But in the 1970s Peebles were in the East section of Division 5 before they started to progress. After being runners up in Division 3 as late as 1989-90 they were promoted to Division 2 as winners.

Under the reconstruction of 1995-6 and 1996-7 they found themselves in Division 2, and it was highly appropriate that their entry to the Border League should occur at this time. They were, after all, ahead of Langholm in Scottish terms.

The very first match, against Selkirk at Philiphaugh, ended in Peebles going down by 28-20, but the Souters had to weather a late Peebles rally that threatened to wipe out the home side's 15 point lead.

The Peebles side which joined the League in 1996.
Back row - Robert Hogarth, President, Mark Stumbles, Kenny Greenshields,
    Gary Whelan, Mark Smith, Calumn Farmer, Willie Napier, Stephen Clapperton,
    Colin Thatcher, David Gray.
Middle row - David Cornwall, Mark Harvey, Alan Jeffrey, Niord McIver
Front row - Stephen Brockie, Michael Millar, Paul Rutherford, Stephen Ferguson,
    Jim Currie, Gordon Wilson, Colin Murray, Colin Kerr.

But the large support which was building up at the fine new ground at The Gytes had to wait less than a month for Peebles' first win in the Border League, a game which is featured. It was a memorable night against Gala which produced a single point home win, greeted by coach Dave Kilshaw as "magnificent".

Peebles went on that year to complete all 14 Border League games, a commitment to their new cause which said a great deal for them, and among the more memorable days and nights were wins over Selkirk and Hawick as well as Gala, all at home, and triumph at Milntown Park, never the easiest of grounds.

Peebles used their first year in the League to blood a lot of youngsters, including Murray Blackstock and Chris Shaw.

Paul Rutherford, off to Melrose ere long, was the leading points scorer of the season and the scorer of the late penalty goal that gave Peebles that first ever Border League win.

Leading the side was Jim Currie, and the Scotland "A" and Scottish Borders prop Steve Ferguson was another solid citizen in the front row.

The next season, 1997-8, saw more Peebles wins, against Kelso and Langholm, and a year later there was only one victory, against Gala, but only ten games in the League could be completed.

Steven Clapperton was the skipper that season, which saw Peebles compensate for their thin showing in the Border League by gaining promotion back to Division 2.

By the end of the century things were picking up again and Peebles had wins over Langholm, Kelso and Hawick to leave themselves in confident mood.

They have a bit of ground to make up on the senior citizens of the League, but the club starts the new millennium in good heart.

The Big Match

Happiness at The Gytes on a Friday Night

It was a dreary old night at The Gytes - at least it started that way - on a Friday evening in October, 1996, when Peebles met Gala in their first ever season in the Border League.

Things had gone well enough for Peebles - a close call with Selkirk in their first match of the competition - but a win was what was needed to settle them alongside the seven other Border clubs.

Gala were the opponents - they had already beaten Hawick and Jed-forest that season - but within minutes of the opening they were being harried and hustled by the home side. Peebles got the formula right, never stopped running all night, and when the chance was there they pounced.

Things didn't go quite right, a try being disallowed, and two kickable penalty chances were missed. But they responded to an enthusiastic crowd, packed on the balcony and enduring the miserable conditions round the ropes.

Colin Kerr's early try converted by Graeme Mutch, and Steven Brockie's score when he pounced on a dropped pass, this time converted by Keith Nisbet, were only the start of a grim night for Gala.

When Jim Currie, showing all the resolution of a captain who could see a glorious win looming up through the murk, ploughed over for a try and an interval score of 19-0 even the most cautious home supporter was sure that Peebles were about to open their Border League account.

Gala's reply was laboured, but Tom Weir gave them a lead and Richie Scott scored. Peebles hit back with a Paul Rutherford penalty - and were playing with all the confidence of a team that could use three successful kickers on one night.

Craig Townsend scored, converted by Chris Paterson. Alan Bell notched his first try for Gala, giving the unhappy Maroons supporters a glimmer of hope in the darkness, and Townsend converted.

Replacement David Changleng slipped over in the left corner after Gala's best handling of the night, and Gala, much to their own surprise, were in front by 24-22.

But the fates had not done with them yet. Peebles were looking for their first win over Gala in the eighth game of an irregular series that had started 114 years earlier. And even although there were understandable doubts about the early games they were certainly playing as well as the oldest home supporter could recall.

Gala sacrificed safety for style when under injury time pressure. Instead of taking the easy option of a touch kick they tried to run out of defence - did they know they were in the lead and the final seconds of the game had arrived ?

Peebles, for the umpteenth time, tackled resolutely, won a penalty, and Rutherford kicked the sweetest of goals to set Peebles on their way in a League they had joined late, but to which they were obviously going to contribute worthily.

The Border League told the S.R.U. in 1987 that the Border clubs were concerned at the continuing extension of representative matches and tours which were bound to have an adverse affect on the sevens and Border League fixtures.

When play resumed in 1946 after the last war the Border League Committee set admission prices for the sevens tournaments as two shillings (ten new pence) for the ground and double for the reserved stand.

Reflections

Memories of the Kelso Breakthrough from Allan "Darkie" Smith of Kelso

A Kelso veteran who played in all three of the club's Border League successes in the 1930s is Allan "Darkie" Smith, who carried on a tradition of commitment to the Black and Whites that had started in the earliest days of Kelso rugby.

With a grandfather known as Strong Bob the blacksmith who played around 130 years ago, and his father also a regular at the turn of the century, Allan Smith came to the Kelso side with a full understanding of what local pride is all about.

Still attending Poynder Park in his ninetieth year, he is not too happy with the emphasis on the physical side of the game today. "In our time there weren't half the injuries there are today in this mauling game.

"Our game was based on foot rushes, but there was still far more open rugby. The scores were smaller, but that's because the defences were good." Having been a full back himself, he had a twinkle in his eye with that observation.

"Darkie" was a member of the Kelso side which won the League for the first time in 1930-1, and recalls the crowds of 3000 which used to throng the field, ignoring the ropes, and getting in the way of the action.

"Once or twice the crowd broke in and if you were trying to field the ball on the touchline you were in amongst the spectators."

Crowds in those days were well behaved on the whole, but the Kelso supporter who was barred from the ground got his marching orders for waving a stick at the referee.

Training on a Pie and a Beer

The personalities of the Kelso side included Tom "Tinkle" Laidlaw, whose enthusiasm for training was lukewarm, to put it mildly. His preparations for any game generally included a pie and a bottle of beer.

"If that bloke had trained he would have played for Scotland", said "Darkie". " He was a natural."

There may have been no professionalism in the thirties, and virtually nothing in the way of sponsorship, but there was one great incentive for young players to progress on the Kelso club scene.

Treasurer Jock Laing ruled that if you were in the first fifteen you were given a high tea at away games, but if you were travelling with the seconds the entertainment was scaled down to a plain tea.

Admittance to the games was at one time as low as two old pence, and little opportunity to spend more, with no bar at Kelso, or indeed at Selkirk where Allan Smith spent a season.

Others in the early days of Kelso rugby were Alex Cameron, whose talent was only recognised when he moved from Kelso to Dunfermline and Walter Forrest, who had to start playing in Hawick before being capped.

Allan Smith recalls the first man to be capped from Kelso, namesake Bob Smith, a giant for those days of around 18 stone. His contribution to the Kelso successes in the Border League of the 1930s was immense.

And the teams that Kelso met in that vintage period at Poynder Park were pretty immense too. From Hawick came Doug Davies and Jock Beattie, from Selkirk Jack Waters, and from Gala Jimmy Ferguson and Henry Polson - big names of big men in a great period of Border rugby.

Allan Smith still remembers their driving forward play, typical of the Border League rugby of the time.

He may have some doubts about the way the game has gone, but as one of Kelso's longest serving players and supporters he would be more than happy if the present Poynder Park side were to top the Border League again.

Old Values Still Needed in League's Future, says Robin Charters, of Hawick, ex President of the S.R.U.

No club has ever been relegated from the Border League. In fact in a hundred years of competition between, at the most, eight clubs, the question of relegation has seldom even been discussed.

One man who considers that this is one of the strengths of the Border League is Robin Charters, the Hawick stalwart who not only played for his country but who went on to be president of the Scottish Rugby Union.

He is realistic enough to know that while there was no relegation one of the reasons was that it would, in the early days, have been very hard to find someone to replace a relegated side.

Now, with Peebles and Berwick coming up in the Border game he sees a widening of the League as the way forward.

"Remember that a hundred years ago there was the travel problem. You could get a horse and buggy, or a charabang on a Saturday morning and get to play at each other's ground - you couldn't do that with Edinburgh games. But it must still have been a hell of a journey coming back from Langholm on a wet November night!"

It's not only as a former President of the S.R.U. that Robin Charters rejects the idea that the Union in the early days was opposed to the formation of the Border League

"I don't think there was any serious falling out between the Union and the Border clubs. The Union had the reputation of being staid and conservative but they still had some very good ideas and the formation of the Border League was one of the ideas they wanted to support."

Where Robin Charters parts company from latter day Murrayfield thinking is in the formation of the two professional sides in the late nineties. "We have done extremely badly in this area as a result of the Union going for these two teams, in an effort to build up their ability.

"The bad side is that they have discarded a district like the South, which has had a very detrimental effect on the whole of the Borders.

"I think the link between the Border clubs and the South will come back in time. The people in the Borders would support the Border Reivers, but not the Edinburgh Reivers."

Robin Charters considers that two teams are not enough to supply the needs of Scotland.

District Rugby the Way Forward

"I am an out and out believer that we must bring back the South district, and all the other districts. I would make them semi professional, bring in as many players qualified for Scotland as possible, and could be afforded.

"That would mean the clubs would not be losing as many players, and the club scene would be built up again, allowing the clubs longer and more frequent use of their players.

"At the top end is Scotland - if Scotland does not do well the money will not come into the game. The Union generates a lot of money that is distributed through the clubs. The Border clubs are getting lots of money that was never there in our day.

"It's not for players, but to deal with the grassroots of the game, secretaries, coaches, grounds, and so forth. That's why we must keep the Scottish team going near the top.

"Run four teams at semi professional level and each area could support its own district."

Looking back at the Border League over the past century, Robin Charters assesses the economic prosperity of the Border towns as having a major impact on the rugby clubs.

"For years Hawick won the Border League and if we didn't win we were considered to be a poor side. It was simply a question of numbers. Hawick had more players, and it had all to do with local prosperity."

He cites the other Border towns as proof of the links between trade and rugby. Langholm started off well, and went downhill because of textile recession.

After the first world war the first town to suffer was Jedburgh with the loss of so much trade.

"Then Gala, Selkirk, and Hawick all suffered when the tweed industry went down. Hosiery kept Hawick going and it was a boom town. But as time rolled on now it's Hawick's turn to suffer with knitwear going down."

Losses with the Modern Game

The old days of Border rugby still mean a lot to Robin Charters. "Despite the economic problems rugby in these days was a great attraction. Townsfolk supported their club - it was a place to go -and there was a wonderful social life. There was a lot of patter with the opposition, and it was great fun.

"But somehow all that has gone in the professional game. We know the game had to change and we had to change with it. I take the view that we call it sport still, but it's not sport.

"Our definition of sport was something else - you played hard and you played to win, but you enjoyed yourself doing it, and you enjoyed mixing after the game with the opposition.

"The fact is that somebody has to come second. Nowadays if you lose no one wants to know you."

Recalling Hawick's great runs in the years after the second world war, Robin Charters talked nostalgically of the fifteen man rugby the Greens featured for so long.

"The backs were told to play to the forwards and the forwards to play to the backs. With their good packs of forwards and the likes of Drew Broatch and Glen Turnbull, Harry Whittaker and Colin Telfer, Hawick had the winning of games."

And mention of the tactical kicking that is missing from today's game draws another nostalgic sigh. "Where are the box kicks, the grubber, now that the players are frightened to kick the ball to touch where they will lose the lineout?

"The changes to the laws that have been made over the last few years have done nothing to help the game. The law makers tried to hard to make an expansive game for players and spectators, but it's not achieved that. It's become a bit of a bore.

"The legislation has been made for the top end of the game where the players are bigger and stronger, but we should try to get back to the old style rugby that made the Border League such a great competition to play in and to watch. We must get back to some of the old ways and the old laws."

And to the future ? He sees the need for co-operation between the Border clubs to help each other. "Sit the clubs down together and agree not to pay for play. At the moment one club makes a move and another tries to counter it. The Border clubs just can't afford to go on like this."

Robin Charters is not alone in seeing a return to the old values which created the League as being the salvation of the future. Maybe the original committee got it right when they set their faces against relegation.

Top Players Needed for the Game Tomorrow says Derek Brown, of Melrose, ex President of the S.R.U.

Back at Melrose after his days as President of the S.R.U. Derek Brown feels that the Border League still has a great role to play in the rugby structure in the South of Scotland.

"It's a great competition, but it's been devalued because of the lack of the top players. I hope it's going to keep going, for if you don't have a competition like that you lose another attraction".

The sportsmanship of the League is one of the features he singled out for praise, recalling the Hawick against Jed-forest match which settled the title as the new century dawned.

Derek Brown feels that much of the bond that draws the Border clubs together came from the First World War, especially the men from the south country who went to Gallipoli together. "My grandfather George was in the war, and my father always said that it unified the Borderers who went with the K.O.S.B. Those who came back carried their links on to the rugby field."

He would like to see other districts in Scotland form leagues similar to the Borders set up. "That would strengthen Scottish rugby. At present there's too big a gap between the professional and the club sides at present, and lots of keen supporters have just gone away. They won't support the professional sides."

But he sees the game as now faster and the players fitter than in the 1950s when he captained Melrose to a Border League triumph. "They train much harder and they're all fit....in my day only 75 per cent were fit."

Even in his playing days there were men in the Melrose side who could see changes looming.

"I remember Charlie Drummond talking to Robin Chisholm and me in the late 1950s - he said eventually it would be the South who would be playing Northampton and Swansea and Leicester.

"Robin Chisholm said - 'it'll not be me - I'll be playing for Melrose', but Charlie could see ahead. He never said it would be professional but he did see how travelling would become so much easier."

Recalling the crowds who watched Border League rugby during his playing time Derek Brown said that when he was about to run on to The Greenyards to play Hawick one day the Melrose trainer Jim Cassie said "There's a crowd like Melrose sevens out there."

Rugby was hard at that time, even for those totally fit, but there were times when even the law could bend a bit to the cause of the game.

"We had played Selkirk in a decider at Philiphaugh to win the Border League and realised that by the time we got back to Melrose it would be ten o'clock and the pubs would be closed.

"But my father, (the late Bob Brown, secretary and president of Melrose) phoned the local police sergeant and explained the situation. 'That's all right, Bob', he was told. 'I'll be in Lilliesleaf tonight so you'll be all right until eleven.' "

The Colourful Characters of Philiphaugh recalled by Graham Bateman of Selkirk

Selkirk's Graham Bateman has been chronicling the Philiphaugh scene for many years. His personal collection of photographs and records have become especially valuable following the disastrous flood of 1975 when so many of the Selkirk minute books were destroyed.

He recalls many of the characters and celebrated players who have given Philiphaugh such a rich heritage.

Pride in Selkirk has always shown through with men like Bert Lawrie around the scene.

When but a teenage player for Selkirk he was called into the South team to replace Billy Nisbet of Melrose against the North at Dundee.

Greatly thrilled, he was sent off superbly kitted out by an equally enthusiastic mother, only to find in Edinburgh that Nisbet had arrived after all to claim his place.

Invited to go on with the South party, Bert Lawrie did a sharp about turn, caught the next train back to the Borders, and turned out for Selkirk that afternoon, scoring two tries in a win against Jed-forest.

And when the new stand at Philiphaugh was built in 1926 Jimmy Liddle, one of Selkirk's legendary back room boys, was appointed to extol its virtues to the many interested visitors.

In his characteristic way he pointed out that the structure was made of "that new stuff, asbestos, and if it was burned tae the grund, it wud still be standin'."

Graham Bateman, who picks out Willie Bryce and Jack Waters as two of the pre-second World War players who typified the Selkirk spirit, recalls both as gentlemen of the game.

But even Jack Waters was moved to remonstrate in a tough game against opponents who could be identified by anyone with a grasp of Border dialect.

Four of Selkirk's Border League stalwarts, all capped for Scotland - Jack Waters, Jim "Basher" Inglis, Jock King and Willie Bryce

Border League rugby was pretty intense in the 1930s - when was it anything else? - and Jack was one of the last to carp about any underhand methods used against him.

But his patience gave way and he was moved to complain when an opponent constantly tugged at his jersey, only for Jack to receive the rejoinder "Ach, ye're better grippit, yow !"

After the war it was characters like the laconic George Downie and the more extrovert Jim "Basher" Inglis who dominated the Philiphaugh scene.

Captain of the club in the big season of 1952-3 George had a simple approach to his role. Leading the pack was "Basher" and all he had to do was to carry out George's instructions "Keep 'em going, old chap".

"Basher" himself contributed richly to the Selkirk scene for more than 50 years, Graham Bateman recalls.

During one League game his second row team mate David Walker couldn't understand how his ear was becoming red raw following packing down at every set scrum.

The mystery was solved only when "Basher" revealed that he had picked up a handful of old time pennies lying on the turf and popped them into the pocket of the baggy pants favoured in these days, with disastrous results to David's ear.

The same "Basher" anticipated the arrival of the modern streaker in a League game where he had his jersey ripped clean off. With no replacement immediately available, to the delight of the spectators, the irrepressible "Basher" carried on till the end of the game.

Graham Bateman tells with some regret the tale of Jock King, the third of the great Selkirk front row.

In the 1950s the team owed much of its success to Jock, one of the most effective hookers of the day, whose international appearances were limited to only four.

His restricted appearances for Scotland were reputed to be the result of accusations of his dangerous swinging in the scrums by a leading former player and authoritative writer on the game.

But when it was too late to add to his caps, Jock received a letter of apology from the self same critic.

Selkirk's contribution to the Border League may have been limited in trophies, but the club has given richly of its characters and gifted players.

A Few Border League Thoughts from John Smail, former Editor, Southern Reporter

As a schoolboy, I would never attend a sporting occasion without my autograph book, and over the years managed to capture the signatures of several international stars. These included All Blacks legend Brian Lochore and England cricket skipper Brian Close.

However, there is one sportsman much closer to home whose autograph remains one of the most prized in my collection - Langholm's evergreen three-quarter Christy Elliot. In his playing days, the 12 times capped internationalist personified everything worthwhile about the Border League, and embodies the competition's enduring appeal.

Having made his debut in the Langholm 1st XV as a strapping 15 year old in 1948, Christy's playing career in the League spanned an incredible four decades (the Milntown worthy finally hanging up his boots in the early 1970s). Such dedication is typical of the loyalty to town and club which the Border League has inspired in generations of local rugby players.

I was lucky enough to experience the Border League both on the playing field and from the Press benches. I turned out in a handful of league fixtures for Selkirk in the late 1970s, and quickly discovered that reporting on matches from the safety of the Press box was an altogether less hazardous affair.

That is, unless you count that infamous Jed-forest v. West of Scotland match at Riverside Park, when the Jed Water burst its banks an hour or so after the final whistle. Everyone in the clubhouse had to be swiftly evacuated as the floodwaters rose, and we found ourselves wading through two feet of icy water up to the town centre.

Unlike the Burnbrae team - who were forced to stay the night at a local hotel - I managed to made it back home at around one a.m., after

Arthur Dorward gets the ball away for Gala against Selkirk at Philiphaugh

police finally re-opened the A.68. Talk about a game receiving saturation coverage !

Another date which sticks out is April 12th, 1988 - the Border League play-off match between Kelso and Jed-forest at The Greenyards. The derby showdown lived up to all expectations, with the Royal Blues just edging out the Tweedsiders to clinch the title.

Seeing the tears flowing down the cheeks of Riverside stalwart Bill Purdie as he stood in the middle of the Jed dressing room after the game will remain one of the abiding memories of my time covering Borders rugby.

Just as many Border league players were privileged to turn out alongside some of the game's greatest figures during those golden years when rugby remained an amateur sport, so I count myself lucky to have covered matches during the hey-day of two legendary Borders rugby scribes.

Bill McLaren's knowledge of the game remains second to none, and his pawky humour, unfailing kindness and unending supply of toffees always made him the ideal companion in any press box.

However, I'm sure Bill would be the first to acknowledge that the contribution made over a period of 60-odd years by Selkirk's Walter Thomson qualified him as the doyen of Borders rugby reporting.

Whether penning articles under the pseudonym of "Fly-Half" (Sunday Post) Ruberslaw (Edinburgh Evening News) or simply in his own newspaper (The Selkirk Saturday Advertiser) Walter brought to his reports and bulletins a freshness of approach and meticulous attention to detail which proved a benchmark for any aspiring rugby journalist.

Travelling by bus and train all over the country to follow the fortunes of local teams, Walter Thomson, perhaps more than any other rugby writer of his generation, helped keep the Border League in the public eye, so ensuring it continued to hold a special place in the affections of Borderers the world over. Rugby, and the Border League in particular, will be forever in his debt.

Hopes and Fears for the Future of the League. from Jack Mitchell, ex President, Gala.

One of Gala's longest serving committeemen, Jack Mitchell, has no doubt about the contribution the Border League has made to rugby in the south of Scotland, but looks to the future with some foreboding.

Secretary of Gala for 16 years from 1951-2 and President from 1971-3, Jack is convinced that the harmonious Border structure was what produced the great South teams.

"The clubs were rivals, but all were very friendly, even off season. There was a family atmosphere and none of that animosity that we sometimes see today."

Singling out Langholm for their contribution to the League, Jack Mitchell said that the work they put in was tremendous. "They scarcely missed a meeting in my time, and they spoke a lot of sense. All of them seemed to have been around for a hundred years, and folk like Jimmy Barnfather were great stalwarts.

"We've lost something nowadays, and I wouldn't bet a hundred pounds on the Border League still being there in the same form in, say, 30 years time."

Jack Mitchell can't see anything changing but for the worse as far as the clubs are concerned. "Taking away the players could kill off the club game, but I hope that Gala can go on playing Hawick as long as the game survives. And I hope that the Border League will continue.

"If the young players continue to come forward, and if the clubs can be given financial recompense when talent is taken away, then there is hope."

The Lighter Side of the League from Bob Burrell of Gala, former international referee, and George Murray, ex referee and Bank of Scotland Border League Secretary

The Border League has produced a rich crop of characters, off the field as well as on it. And Border referees have had to take their share of banter from round the ropes, often, not surprisingly, at Langholm.

Gala's Bob Burrell was at Milntown one day and officiating in a game where one of his touch judges was wearing an eye patch.

"How are we gaun tae win the day, wi' a touch judge wi' yin e'e? " inquired a voice from the waterside crowd. "Aye, and a referee wi' nane", replied his pal.

And heckled at one Border ground Bob heard the complaint - "You don't know the rules, ref." Unwisely Bob thought he would have the last word and shouted back - "We don't play to rules, we call them laws!"

"Well, you don't know the bloody laws either," was the speedy response.

Border League secretary George Murray is another former player and referee who has had his moments to remember with local supporters.......and players.

At Riverside Park one day the home crowd was none too happy with his refereeing in a match against Hawick. Jim Renwick was about to take a long kick at goal from the touch line when the ball fell over.

"Can I pick it up, ref?" asked Jim. "Leave it, Jim," said a voice from the home crowd. "Let Murray pick it up. He's done everything else for you today."

But George did get the final word in his last game at Philiphaugh. Awarding a penalty against Cyril Johnston, the redoubtable Langholm scrum half, for an unspecified offence, he was questioned as to his motifs. "That's for all the trouble you've given me over the past 15 years", said George, and there was no reply to that.

Border League secretary George Murray is the referee in this Gala- Hawick tie which features many outstanding players of the 1960s, including Hugh McLeod, Glen Turnbull, Brian King, George Stevenson, Rob Valentine, Drew Broatch and Derek Grant of Hawick, and Nat Carson, Jock Turner, Tom Scott and Mike Brunton of Gala.

Memories from the Cuttings Book
By Atholl Innes, Editor, The Border Telegraph

Delving through the old newspaper files in "The Border Telegraph" office, I came across a photograph of Jim Renwick, one of the finest players ever to pull on a rugby jersey for club and country.

Jim was playing in a Netherdale derby against Gala, and it was not Jim's side-step in the picture that grabbed my attention, but the huge crowd which packed the banking opposite the main stand. There was barely elbow room.

Perhaps many travelled by train to Galashiels, and if stories handed down the years are to be believed, the crowds would have dispersed long before the final whistle if the Greens had been on the receiving end.

The same would be said of Gala supporters in a similar situation at Mansfield Park!

Now I have to confess to having been born in Galashiels, but that does not necessarily make me a Gala man as I was brought up three miles away in the principality which is Clovenfords, home of that great Maroons stalwart Peter Dods.

Peter, like Jim Renwick, was a huge credit to Borders rugby, and I recall one day standing on the wide open spaces at Mansfield Park where he scored a try to give Gala a rare victory over their greatest rivals.

My Border League memories take me back further and a game I remember for the scoreline rather than the performance. It was 65-8 for Hawick, or close to that!

Yet perhaps my best memories are of comments from the terraces. Away back tae Melrose, ref! He's offside man; Open yer eeen, Burrell (reference to another great character, Bob Burrell); Gee him a lift-up (Gary Parker chatting with Ian Barnes).

One of the most pleasing aspects of working in a newspaper office is the convenience of delving into the old copies, a history of Border League rugby on its own.

March 1959 - Selkirk, having one of their worst ever seasons, offered no challenge to Melrose at Philiphaugh. (Incidentally, Langholm topped the Border League with 87 per cent).

February 1965 - The Braw Lads must be wondering if their luck is ever going to change at Mansfield Park (after D. S. Paterson injured his collarbone).

October 1965 - There was a lot of mishandling and misdirected kicks (Kelso v. Melrose).

March 1969 - The forwards played an extremely robust and forceful game. It was a bruising game (Kelso v. Gala)

December 1969 - Telfer and his men could not be faulted for the effort (Melrose v. Hawick).

Writing styles have changed over the years.

On December 27, 1949, the "Border Telegraph" reported: "Selkirk ended a run of defeats by playing a drawn game. The Philiphaugh players showed a welcome liveliness throughout the whole game, and this was particularly obvious at a late stage in the game when a clever interception by Dalgleish almost placed Selkirk in a position which their opponents would not have countered."

Today's reports tend to focus on quotes from the captains and team managers with the game itself taking a back seat. But like the Border League, newspapers have seen many changes down the century. Our duty remains to report on games well into the next century when a "new" Dods, Renwick, Stevenson, Rutherford, Jeffrey will emerge. And no doubt the banter from the terraces will just be the same.

SPONSORS' SUPPORT FOR BORDER RUGBY

The pages of the Border League story have to be turned to recent years to find the background to one of the most influential factors in the running of today's game - sponsorship.

The League was early into this development, and secured the support of Scotch Beef from 1987 to 1990. Since then the Bank of Scotland have held the title to the League, providing, as did their predecessors, financial assistance to the clubs and considerable support in social functions.

A refinement from the earliest days is the award of cash for individual tries and a lump sum to the team with the leading try scorer.

The District League, too, has been supported by companies anxious to be associated with the Borders' prime sport.

Hart Builders backed the District League for four years until 1991, being succeeded by the Solicitors Property Centres (Borders) who supported the competition until 1997.

The Border sevens tournaments received great support through the creation of the Kings of the Sevens competition originated by Radio Borders, and backed by Kleenex Tissues and latterly by Lowland Insurance Brokers, Ltd.

The League's indebtedness to all these companies, and the others who have contributed to the wellbeing of the game in the Borders through the sevens and other fixtures, is acknowledged with gratitude by the committee and the member clubs.

THE DISTRICT LEAGUE

The make-up of the senior league has changed little over the century, but it's been a very different matter in the Border District League, set up to provide a similar competition for the junior and second fifteens in the Borders.

Such was the popularity of the league that in the 1920s it was found necessary to restrict the numbers seeking admittance. The names of the sides approved for competition in 1920-1 were Hawick "A", Hawick Waverley, Hawick Albion, Gala "A", Gala Star, Gala Trinity, Jed-forest "A", Selkirk "A", Melrose "A", Kelso "A", Walkerburn and Earlston.

Duns, Annan, Berwick, Peebles, Langholm "A" and Gala Forest are only some of the other sides which have featured in the District League, most of them still thriving at the end of the century, and some in even more exalted company.

Whereas only seven names appear on the honours board of the senior league, no fewer than 16 teams are credited as champions among the juniors.

The restructuring of senior clubs, the merging of some junior sides and the complete disappearance of others, explains the variety of names, with such former illustrious sides as Gala Hearts and Hawick Albion having had only a brief period in the Border story.

The main strand that emerges with the juniors, as with the seniors, is the strength of Hawick rugby. The independent clubs along Teviotside have picked up no fewer than 46 titles, fit comparison with the senior side's 44.

The Gala clubs, the Star, the Y.M. and Gala "A", have a total of 19, and the remaining titles are shared between Melrose "A" or 2nds, Selkirk "A", Kelso "A", Jed-forest "A" and Walkerburn, with none of them succeeding more than three times.

The outstanding team in the 80 competitions has been Hawick Linden, with 11 wins. From their first success in the 1930s they have delivered consistently and remain the only independent club to have won three titles in a row. Their win in 1969-70 produced no fewer than 624 points, including 120 tries, one of the outstanding feats of Borders junior rugby.

Scottish Borders Council Convener Drew Tulley (second left) hands over the Centenary Trophy to current the Border League President Jock Scott of Langholm (second right). In attendance Tom Henderson of Selkirk (far left) and Henry Aitchison of Kelso (centre) the two oldest surviving ex-presidents and League secretary George Murray (far right).

The trophy will be presented to the team winning the League in season 2000-01

BORDER LEAGUE PRESIDENTS

Years	Name	Club	Years	Name	Club
1901-1902			1955-1956	G. Cairns	Hawick
1902-1903			1956-1957	J. R. B. Wilson	Jed-Forest
1903-1904			1957-1958	R. Michie	Melrose
1904-1905			1958-1959	H. S. P. Monro	Langholm
1905-1906	A. Turnbull	Hawick	1959-1960	R. M. Grieve	Kelso
1906-1907			1960-1961	R. C. N. Rankine	Selkirk
1907-1908			1961-1962	J. H. Ferguson	Gala
1908-1909			1962-1963	J. G. Landles	Hawick
1909-1910			1963-1964	Dr. G. W. Balfour	Jed-Forest
1910-1911	C. J. N. Fleming	Melrose	1964-1965	T. D. Wight	Melrose
1911-1912	G. S. Scott	Selkirk	1965-1966	A. Irving	Langholm
1912-1913	A. D. Lawson	Gala	1966-1967	J. Grieve	Kelso
1913-1914	A. Brown	Melrose	1967-1968	W. Brownlee	Selkirk
1914-1919	Great War		1968-1969	R. G. Nicholson	Gala
1919-1920	W. Laidlaw	Jed-Forest	1969-1970	J. C. Robertson	Hawick
1920-1921	J. McGeorge	Langholm	1970-1971	R. C. Maxwell	Jed-Forest
1921-1922	T. Black	Kelso	1971-1972	R. G. Baird	Kelso
1922-1923	J. B. Hall	Selkirk	1972-1973	D. M. Hogg	Melrose
1923-1924	A. S. Park	Gala	1973-1974	J. G. Barnfather	Langholm
1924-1925	G. L. McDonald	Hawick	1974-1975	R. Lawrie	Selkirk
1925-1926	J. T. Mabon	Jed-Forest	1975-1976	T. P. Carruthers	Gala
1926-1927	W. M. Henderson	Melrose	1976-1977	G. Penman	Hawick
1927-1928	R. Hope	Kelso	1977-1978	J. R. Lauder	Jed-Forest
1928-1929	W. H. Lawrie	Selkirk	1978-1979	J. S. Forsyth	Kelso
1929-1930	W. McCrirrick	Gala	1979-1980	G. D. M. Brown	Melrose
1930-1931	J. R. Morgan	Hawick	1980-1981	J. Telford	Langholm
1931-1932	Dr. C. S. Nimmo	Jed-Forest	1981-1982	C. Bell	Selkirk
1932-1933	A. G. Lyal	Melrose	1982-1983	T. Purves	Gala
1933-1934	R. Hope	Kelso	1983-1984	H. F. McLeod	Hawick
1934-1935	A. McDonald	Selkirk	1984-1985	W. Miller	Jed-Forest
1935-1936	J. Brown	Gala	1985-1986	W. S. Forbes	Kelso
1936-1937	J. Park	Hawick	1986-1987	A. Smith	Langholm
1937-1938	J. T. Mabon	Jed-Forest	1987-1988	D. A. Hogg	Melrose
1938-1939	J. Macgregor	Melrose	1988-1989	J. M. Inglis	Selkirk
1939-1940	J. Graham	Kelso	1989-1990	R. P. Burrell	Gala
1940-1945	Second World War		1990-1991	W. R. Scott	Hawick
1945-1946	J. Graham	Kelso	1991-1992	G. R. Miller	Jed-Forest
1946-1947	J. A. T. Beattie	Selkirk	1992-1993	A. L. Mole	Kelso
1947-1948	J. E. Liddle	Gala	1993-1994	J. Balmer	Langholm
1948-1949	R. L. Scott	Hawick	1994-1995	T. J. McLeish	Melrose
1949-1950	R. Lunn	Jed-Forest	1995-1996	W. N. Douglas	Selkirk
1950-1951	H. McCulloch	Melrose	1996-1997	J. Gilchrist	Gala
1951-1952	A. Scott	Langholm	1997-1998	R. Chrystie	Hawick
1952-1953	H. A. Aitchison	Kelso	1998-1999	J. Moody	Jed-Forest
1953-1954	T. Henderson	Selkirk	1999-2000	N. T. Anderson	Kelso
1954-1955	W. Watt	Gala	2000-2001	J. Scott	Langholm

BORDER LEAGUE SECRETARIES & TREASURERS

Years	Name	Club	Years	Name	Club
1906-	J. E. Fairbairn	Melrose			
-1912	G. Stewart	Jed-Forest	1926-1952	R. J. Hogg	Gala
1912-1919	J. Glendinning	Hawick	1952-1963	A. E. Bunyan	Gala
1919-1921	A. Arnott	Gala	1963-1971	T. P. Carruthers	Gala
1921-1923	T. A. Hume	Selkirk	1971-1989	J. C. Robertson	Hawick
1923-1926	W. Lunn	Jed-Forest	1990-	G. G. Murray	Kelso

BORDER LEAGUE CHAMPIONS

1901-02—Hawick
1902-03—Jedforest
1903-04—Jedforest
1904-05—Jedforest
1905-06—Gala
1906-07—Jedforest
(Fist year of Cup)
1907-08—Jedforest
(after play-off
with Hawick at Melrose)
1908-09—Hawick
(after play-off
with Jedforest)
1909-10—Hawick
and Jedforest tie
(No deciding game played)
1910-11—Melrose
(after play-off
with Hawick at Jedburgh)
1911-12—Hawick
1912-13—Hawick
1913-14—Hawick
First World War
1919-20—Jedforest
1920-21—Hawick
(after play-off
with Jedforest at Melrose)
1921-22—Gala
1922-23—Hawick
1923-24—Hawick
1924-25—Hawick

1925-26—Hawick
(after play-off
with Kelso at Melrose)
1926-27—Hawick
1927-28—Hawick
1928-29—Hawick
1929-30—Hawick
1930-31—Kelso
1931-32—Hawick
1932-33—Unfinished
1933-34—Kelso
1934-35—Selkirk
1935-36—Unfinished
1936-37—Kelso
1937-38—Selkirk
1938-39—Melrose
1946-47—Void
1947-48—Void
1948-49—Hawick
1949-50—Gala
and Melrose (tie)
1950-51—Hawick
1951-52—Void
1952-53—Selkirk
1953-54—Melrose
1954-55—Hawick
1955-56—Hawick
1956-57—Jedforest
1957-58—Melrose
1958-59—Langholm
1959-60—Hawick
1960-61—Hawick
1961-62—Hawick
1962-63—Melrose
1963-64—Hawick
1964-65—Hawick
1965-66—Hawick
1966-67—Gala
1967-68—Hawick
1968-69—Hawick
1969-70—Hawick
1970-71—Melrose
1971-72—Hawick
1972-73—Hawick
1973-74—Hawick

1974-75—Hawick
1975-76—Hawick
1976-77—Hawick
1977-78—Hawick
1978-79—Hawick
1979-80—Gala
1980-81—Gala
1981-82—Hawick
1982-83—Hawick
1983-84—Hawick
1984-85—Hawick
1985-86—Kelso
1986-87—Kelso
1987-88—Jedforest
(after play-off with
Kelso at Melrose)
1988-89—Hawick
1989-90—Melrose
1990-91—Melrose
1991-92—Melrose
1992-93—Melrose
1993-94—Melrose
1994-95—Jed-Forest
1995-96—Hawick
1996-97—Melrose
1997-98—Gala
1998-99—Melrose
1999-2000—Hawick
(after play-off with
Jedforest at Melrose)

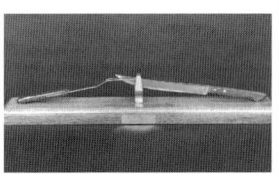

The trophy presented by Scotch Beef, first sponsors of the League, which is now retained by Melrose

The Bank of Scotland have presented trophies to winning sides in the League

BORDER DISTRICT LEAGUE CHAMPIONS

1906-7—Gala Hearts
1907-8—Gala Hearts
1908-9—Hawick
1909-10—Jed-Forest
1910-11—Gala Hearts
1911-12—Hawick A
1912-13—Walkerburn
1913-14—Hawick A
First World War
1920-21—Hk. Albion
1921-22—Hk. Albion
1922-23—Hk. Albion
1923-24—Hawick A
1924-25—Hawick A
1925-26—Hawick A
1926-27—Hawick A
1927-28—Hawick Y.M.C.A.
1928-29—Selkirk A
1929-30—Hawick Linden
1930-31—Gala YM
1931-32— Gala YM
1932-33—Hawick A
1933-34—Gala A
1934-35—Gala Star
1935-36—Gala Star
1936-37—Hawick Linden
1937-38—Gala Star
1938-39—Gala Star
Second World War
1947-48—Hawick Linden
1948-49—Hawick Trades
1949-50—Hawick Trades
1950-51—Hawick Linden
1951-52—Void
1952-53—Melrose A
1953-54—Hawick Linden
1954-55—Melrose A
1955-56—Hawick YM
1956-57—Gala YM
1957-58—Gala YM
1958-59—Hawick YM

1959-60—Kelso A
1960-61—Hawick YM
1961-62—Hawick Trades
1962-63—Void
1963-64—Hawick Trades
1964-65—Hawick Trades
1965-66—Hawick YM
1966-67—Hk. Harlequins
1967-68—Hawick Linden
1968-69—Hawick Linden
1969-70—Hawick Linden
1970-71—Hawick YM
1971-72—Hawick Trades
1972-73—Hawick Linden
1973-74—Hawick YM
1974-75—Gala A
1975-76—Hawick Linden
1976-77—Selkirk A
1977-78—Kelso A
1978-79—Gala A
1979-80—Kelso A
1980-81—Hawick Linden
1981-82—Hawick YM
1982-83—Gala YM
1983-84—Gala YM
1984-85—Hawick YM
1985-86—Hk. Harlequins
1986-87—Hawick Linden
1987-88—Jed-Forest A
1988-89—Hawick YM
1989-90—Hk. Trades
1990-91—Gala Star
1991-92—Gala YM
1992-93—Gala YM
1993-94—Hawick Trades
1994-95—Gala Star
1995-96—Hawick Trades
1996-97—Kelso A
1997-98—Melrose A
1998-99—Melrose A
1999-2000—Jed-Forest A